The Mother Who Loves You

A MEMORIAL

Other books by Anne Urne

COMMUNION OF SAINTS – Inspired by St. Therese

TRUST ME – the Untold Story of Mary Magdalene

A SPIRITUAL TRILOGY

- ❖ *Way Beyond The River*
- ❖ *The Walls Came Tumbling Down*
- ❖ *It Came to Pass*

SPIRITUAL TRILOGY

See Youtube videos:

Interview of Anne Urne by Dyana Jean about *Trust Me*
http://www.youtube.com/watch?feature=player_embedded&v=d5HrJ4wrOXc

Communion of Saints Video Preview by Media3
http://www.youtube.com/watch?v=3xVQ7RH2WEc&feature=em-share_video_user

WEBSITES AND BLOGS

media3.cc/Trust_me.htm
Amazon.com – Anne Urne

boispublishing.blogspot.com
anneurne.blogspot.com

FACEBOOK PAGES
Anne Urne
BOIS Publications

The Mother Who Loves You

A MEMORIAL

ANNE URNE

BOIS PUBLICATIONS /OKLAHOMA CITY, OKLAHOMA

Published by BOIS Publications,
5411 Colfax Place, Oklahoma City, Oklahoma 73112.

Printed in the United States of America

Cover Photographer: Anne Urne
Photo: Pieta of Mary holding the body of Jesus with Mary
Magdalene weeping at her feet taken at the entrance to the
Grotto of Mary Magdalene in Sainte-Baume, Aix-en-
Provence, France

Interior Photos by Anne Thomas and Susan McCubbin
Digitally formatted by Media 3, Sausalito, CA
http://www.media3.cc/

Library of Congress Cataloging-in-Publication Data

Urne, Anne.

The Mother Who Loves You: A Memorial

Library of Congress Control Number: 2013900114

First Printing: January 21, 2013

10 9 8 7 6 5 4 3 2 1

ISBN 978-0-9727967-4-3

First Edition

CONTENTS

ACKNOWLEDGEMENTS

To Malakai
For we are the children of saints
Honor thy mother all the days of her life.

It is honourable to reveal and confess the works
of God and publish all his wonderful works.

Tobias

While I was in the process of writing the book, *Communion of Saints Inspired by St. Therese,* my great-grandson Malakai was conceived. I am certain that on the day he entered this world a saint was born to my beloved grandson, Casey, and his beautiful bride, Ina.

Malakai was born on a very special day, October 1st, the feast day of my spiritual guide and patron saint, Therese of Lisieux.

What joy you bring into this world my beautiful great grandchild; with the most charming smile, wink and a coo you fill the world with your wonder.

Anne Urne

TAN FAIRY

Tan Fairy was the only one my Grandpa said was a boy
He loved to run, jump and play, just like a bouncing toy
He never stopped, he hardly slept
He just kept going every day
The one thing he wanted most
Was just to hear the others say
"Hey there tan fairy
My how you have grown
And your color is a deeper tan."
You see he no longer wanted to be seen as a boy
But to be seen as a man
Now Grandpa said to Tan Fairy
"There's lots of time to grow
For being seen as a man
There's much wisdom you must know
God gave this to King Solomon
It's written in proverbs
And if you learn and live by these
A man all will observe."
Now Tan Fairy is a man
And a fool he never seems to be
For he lives by God's wisdom
For all others now can see
You see Tan Fairy listened and followed Grandpa's advice
And he did grow into a man that is gentle, wise and nice.

Fairies Sprites and Trolls, Leprechaun and Moles
By Marcia Christy

This book is dedicated to my mother in heaven.
Marjorie Griswold

Mom proudly served in the U.S. Army in WWII,
Worked on the Manhattan Project and was presented a
Certificate signed by Henry L. Stimson,
U.S. Secretary of War on 6 August 1945.

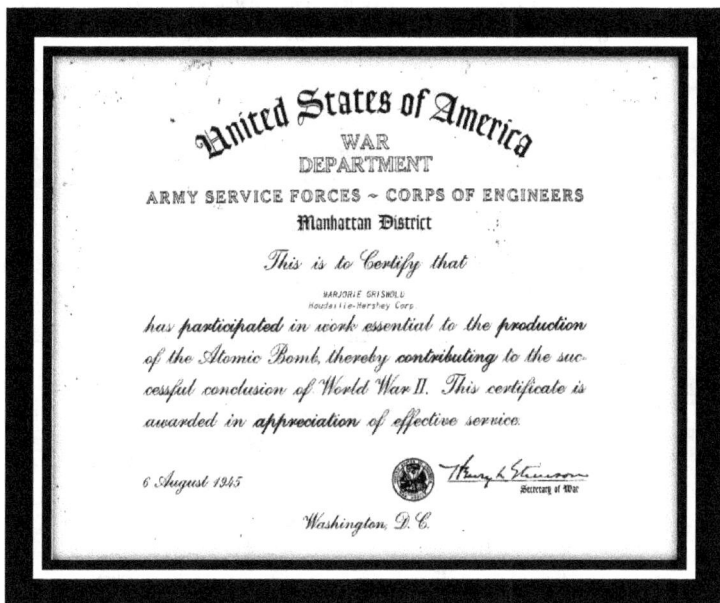

United States of America
WAR
DEPARTMENT
ARMY SERVICE FORCES ~ CORPS OF ENGINEERS
Manhattan District

This is to Certify that

MARJORIE GRISWOLD
Houdaille-Hershey Corp

has participated in work essential to the production
of the Atomic Bomb, thereby contributing to the suc-
cessful conclusion of World War II. This certificate is
awarded in appreciation of effective service.

6 August 1945   Henry L. Stimson
                                    Secretary of War

Washington, D.C.

Marjorie A. McMahon Griswold
11/04/1924 to 04/30/2009

Matriarch and last full blooded Irishwoman in our family.

Mom's grandmother, Brigitte Barry, came over on a boat from Ireland at age 16, married a McMahon from Ireland and had five sons.

Son Michael married Irishwoman Pearl and had two daughters and a son: Marjorie, Marilyn and Richard.

Marjorie married full blooded Englishman John and gave birth to two daughters. She was soon widowed and left alone to raise her two very young girls.

The entire family is so proud of our strong and loving matriarch. She won an academic scholarship to St. Therese Academy in Decatur, Illinois where the sisters advised she had tested as genius. She excelled in chemistry and later worked on the Manhattan Project.

Mom's sense of adventure, twinkling green Irish eyes and unparalleled love for her children forged a family bond that has never been broken. It continues to this day extending to her fourth generation – and we know she always watches over all of us from heaven.

This is a tribute to my mother who loves us.

Anne Married and had a daughter Michelle	Marcia Married and had a daughter Christine and son, John

Michelle Married and had one son Casey	Christine Married and had 3 children: Lindsay, Justin & Lauren	John Married and had one daughter Amanda

Casey married and had a son Malakai	Lindsay married and had a daughter Kayden Michelle

Mom's great great-grandchildren born in 2013

xii

THE REWARDS OF WISDOM

Wisdom instructs her children and admonishes those who seek her. He who loves her loves life, those who seek her out win her favor. He who holds her fast inherits glory; wherever he dwells, the Lord bestows blessings.

Those who serve her serve the Holy One; those who love her, the Lord loves; He who obeys her judges nations; he who hearkens to her dwells in her inmost chambers. If one trusts her, he will possess her; his descendants too will inherit her.

She walks with him as a stranger, and at first she puts him to the test; fear and dread she brings upon him and tries him with her discipline; with her precepts she puts him to the proof, until his heart is fully with her.

Then she comes back to bring him happiness and reveals her secrets to him. But if he fails her, she will abandon him and deliver him into the hands of despoilers.

Sirach 4: 11

*A great anxiety has God allotted and a heavy yoke, to the sons of men; from the day one leaves his mother's womb to the day he returns to **the mother of all the living**.*

Sirach 40:1

*And the man called his wife, Eve, because she was **the mother of all the living**.*

Genesis 3:20

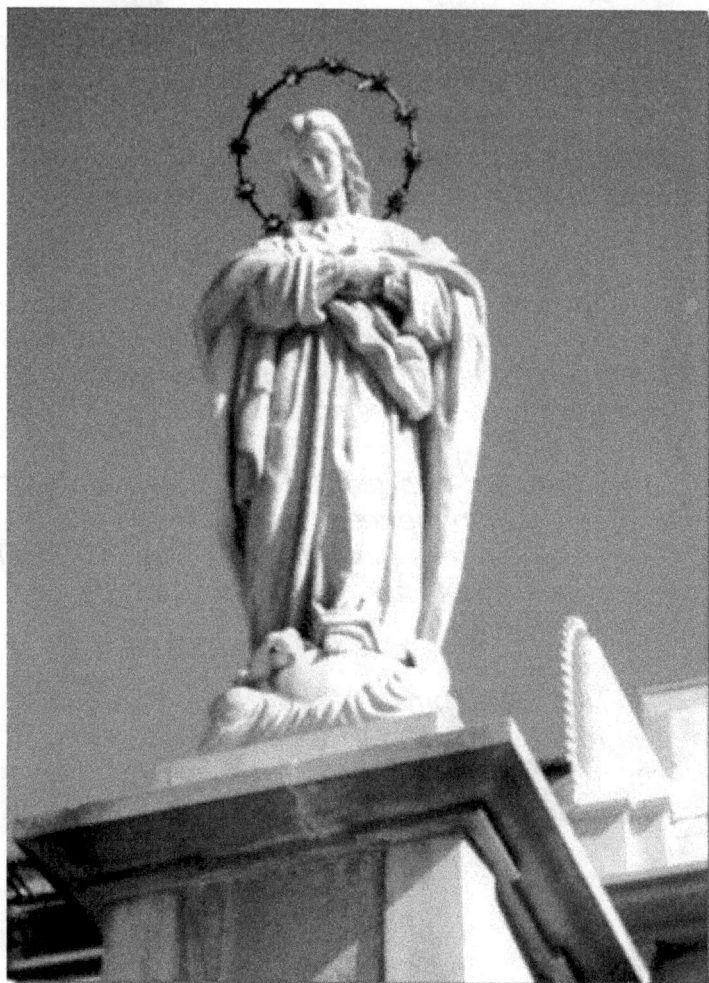

PROLOGUE

There is a song that continues to play in my mind and will not relent until I get out of the bed at 3 a.m. and obey my inner voice that urges me to rise up and write. The melodic words that keep repeating are:

Your love keeps lifting me higher than I've ever been lifted before.

Oh, what trials I have been going through from a subtle and cumulative work related injury. I am still reeling from the effects caused by overuse of a computer mouse.

I work as a paralegal at a downtown law firm and was assigned to a case that had massive document production - over a third of a million pages! It is hard to imagine, but this case was highly unusual and document intensive.

My task was to find information for the attorney and to accomplish that task involved the constant rotation of my arm while simultaneous clicking and scrolling the mouse with my index finger in order to review the myriads of pages.

For two weeks my focus was on nothing other than accomplishing this nearly impossible feat; until one day my finger stopped working. I could no longer move it.

I equate my injury to that of a train wreck where cars derail so much further down the track that the entirety of the wreckage is beyond view.

My initial concern was that my index finger on my dominant hand was swollen, stiff and painful. As I sought medical treatment for my now diagnosed trigger finger I also began to realize the entirety of the damage. Just like derailing train cars, the extent of my damage was unfortunately not limited to just my finger. My arm and neck were also stiff and painful. And, no it didn't stop at my neck. The damage continued on up and into my jaw and caused a TMJ disorder affecting my bite and requiring the attention of another specialist who crafted acrylic and wire splints that attached to my upper and lower teeth to hold my jaw in place. To my horror I learned from the hand and jaw specialists that my damages are irreversible and permanent.

Meanwhile my wonderful family osteopathic physician continues to treat my shoulder and neck pain with an electric muscle stimulator, moist heat, manipulation, muscle relaxers and anti-inflammatories. Now I am under the care of a hand surgeon, a TMJ specialist and continuing treatment with my family physician. Needless to say I am not a happy girl. All I can think about is that this damage is permanent. My hands have always been the tools of my trade; I could type 120 words per minute. Now my right index finger has an enlarged joint where it connects to my hand and it twists to the right overlapping my middle finger. Sleeping with a mouthful of acrylic fastened to my upper teeth at night and wearing another one on my bottom teeth during the day is neither pleasant nor attractive.

In addition to these maladies, I also have to deal with the stand firm against all claims insurance company and their offensive representative who sets me up with their hand specialist and then shoots off a letter denying payment for any further treatment with my family physician. The company refuses to even acknowledge that I am in need of specialized treatment for my jaw; and, of course, their hand surgeon determined that nothing can be done for my permanently damaged finger. So, now the insurance company pronounces that I no longer require medical care!

With a snap of their fingers the insurance company has denied any liability for damage that extends beyond my hand.

Further, *if I believe that I need additional doctors to treat me, I must make a formal request by filing a claim with the courts,* they declared in a letter. So now I must engage a lawyer to seek treatment.

Gee, can I have any more fun?

Wait - there's more . . . and there is a lesson to be learned as a spiritual and poignant story unfolds revealing *the Mother who loves you.*

CHAPTER ONE

THE VOICE

Not long after finishing my most prized book *Communion of Saints Inspired by St. Therese* which truly convinced me that I have the recipe for living my heaven on earth, I realize that I cannot manifest that divine dessert unless I combine the ingredients and actually prepare the delightful delicacy that my soul longs to taste.

In the midst of my current trials over the maladies that manifested from a traumatic, dramatic and cumulative finger injury, came a most welcome note from the Sisters of Benedict thanking me for my support and including a short prayer and song to Mother Mary.

A flood of joy and peace filled my soul as I read the prayer to Mother Mary and I was reminded of her words that came to me very early one morning many years ago.

Yes, I heard God's voice in answer to a prayer and that is an experience which I will never forget. It occurred shortly after my sister passed away at the young age of forty-six, and I was especially angry over her loss because it brought such pain to her children.

After long prayers and tears in the hours before dawn as I prayed in my bed, I remember telling God of my anger in not being able to console my niece, Christine. In the midst of this anguished prayer God answered me and that answer brought profound relief to my soul.

My anger melted away in tears of relief when I heard God answer me, saying:

"You don't know how I can comfort her!"

He then continued with the most loving and profound statement:

"I am the Father who created you and
the Mother who loves you."

Immediately following these words, that male voice changed gender and I heard my very own mother's voice speak to me:

"Why Anne, I have always been there for you."

I understood that it was still God who was speaking to me, even though the voice changed from masculine to feminine and became the voice of my own mother. For God showed me in a profound moment of tenderness that He was truly my Father and my Mother!

And, by speaking to me in the voice of my very own dear mother, God was conveying His great love for me in a way I could understand. In fact, I believe that a mother's love is the greatest love we know on this earth, and it is beyond our imagination and capacity to understand the magnitude of God's love for us.

With such a profound repertoire of words from my God, Father and Mother, I have great confidence that their love is always present to bring me safely through whatever trials present and bring me to a higher place of peace and joy. God is that ever-present power of love that *lifts me higher than I have ever been lifted before.*

"Oh thank you Mother for your loving reassurance that I am not alone during my trials. You are here and all will turn out well."

Our Lady of the Smile, who healed young Therese
Statue of Mary is in the National Shrine of St. Therese

CHAPTER TWO

THE WRECK

November 8, 2011 - Oklahoma City

This particular Monday morning marks the day that changed my life and pointed me in a direction that took me down a dark, spiraling and unfamiliar path of physical calamities and spiritual struggles.

It all began with an injury to my right index finger that was diagnosed as tenosynovitis, more commonly known as a trigger finger. As earlier described, my injuries included a multitude of affected areas requiring treatment by varied specialists with resultant legal battles to pursue a judicial remedy.

The initial treatment to my finger was excruciatingly painful when the hand specialist pulled out a very long needle and stabbed it into the inside of my hand at the base of my finger to inject it with steroids. He advised this should help loosen up the tendons, however, my knuckle joint now has arthritis and the swelling may never dissipate.

This was the beginning of the calamity that ensued. I surely empathized with Job as my injuries continued to mount. My TMJ disorder is yet another result of the undue stress placed upon my finger, hand, arm and shoulder during the two-week period of prolonged repetitive movements; clicking, scrolling and rotating a computer mouse to accomplish an assigned task at the law office where I am employed.

The insurance company continues to deny any liability to this day other than my permanently damaged finger. Anger was surely getting a foothold as the insurer continued to deny my injuries and the battle began. I was forced to engage an attorney to pursue payment of my medical bills through the workers' compensation court while undergoing treatment by several doctors with different specialties for my various injured body parts.

During the months that ensued I felt like a dog chasing his tail and I had turned into a shrew with my Irish temper flaring, my mood spiraling downward and my blood pressure rising to new heights.

Here I was, writing the most wonderfully inspired story of St. Therese in *Communion of Saints*, and I am behaving like a demon from hell! Can it get any worse?

"Oh, please God, No!"

For what I fear overtakes me, and what I shrink from comes upon me, I have no peace nor ease; I have no rest, for trouble comes!

Job 5:25

CHAPTER THREE

SURRENDER

I am continually reminded of the message that I received while completing my book about the saints. I re-read the words written centuries ago by a French priest, Father Caussade, who speaks of abandoning oneself to God's inspiration and living in self-surrender to God's will.

He communicates His will fully to it (the heart), because His love has given it an infinite capacity by emptying it of all created things and making it capable of union with God.

The Joy of Full Surrender
A Spiritual Classic by
Jean-Pierre de Caussade

I have known communion with God and experienced cherished moments in communion with the saints, so how can I be so stupid as to not understand what is being demanded of me in this situation of ongoing and various trials?

Again, I have the recipe, but have not made the dessert! I know to rejoice in trials which my beloved St. James taught in his Gospel; and I know I must surrender and completely trust God with all confidence and love which I learned from St. Therese, and which was further emphasized by Father Caussade's words. I even wrote the book, *Trust Me*. So why am I failing so miserably at letting go and letting God? I know beyond any doubt that I can rely on all the saints to come to my aid, and I know that my God who loves me is always near and eager to help me. I must surrender the roadblocks to my heavenly blessings.

I am sure this chapter of my life is yet another lesson in overcoming life's trials. I still have much to learn, so it is with great pleasure and anticipation that I look forward to the unfolding of this new book.

I know and understand that just as my injuries and resultant anger have taken me down a dark and slippery slope towards a hellish pit; the hand of God is also here to rescue me. The Father who created me and the Mother who loves me are always present. That is why I never cease praying for divine guidance and calling on the intercession of my wonderful saints. I know that I need all the help I can muster to lift me higher than the walls I have thrown up in anger which are preventing my ascent to higher living.

The lessons are cascading down from heaven simultaneously with the medical maladies which manifested in concert with my repetitive stress injury. Together I believe both the injuries and the lessons will work together in a chain like reaction to bring me closer to God. The major hurdle will be getting me out of God's way!

For every ugly emotional reaction I have embraced and every cursing word I have uttered in my seemingly helpless and hopeless trials, I never lose sight of the lessons of life that I have already learned and the promises that have been handed down through the prophets and saints from the beginning of time.

I look to Job and understand that I need to shut my mouth. Then, I have a daughter whom I describe as a human Geiger counter for her detection of the slightest negative movements. Michelle will be talking to me on the phone and if I go off on a negative tangent about the bad things - she abruptly stops me short, telling me to stop uttering such negative remarks, gives me a short and brief antidote and gets off the phone. She is so sensitive to negativity because she is wise beyond her years in spiritual wisdom. She is my pride and joy. An accomplished athlete and former gymnast, Michelle is my spiritual warrior. And to her credit she lives a wonderful life and she is the most beautiful strawberry blonde that ever walked this earth - as far as I am concerned - all five feet of her powerful self!

It is one thing to know God and do right when all is going well, but it is quite another feat to surrender all the fear, anger and negative thoughts and emotions that accompany various trials. I have succeeded many times in overcoming emotional assaults, but I find myself in new territory experiencing for the very first time an assault on my physical body. And, I have been reacting to this unfamiliar assault in all the wrong ways.

Through it all I never relinquish my faith in God, even when reacting negatively. I know the basics and I am coming to grips with this battle. I may take one step forward and two steps back, but I will never surrender in defeat. Instead I will strive to surrender my every negative thought, emotion and utterance to the Lord who has already won all of my battles. Then, like Job, I will find peace for my restless soul.

God restored the fortunes of Job when he finally covered his mouth and then prayed for his friends. God even increased all that Job had twofold.

With promises like that, how can I possibly continue in my self-pity, resentment and anger? I will refocus my sights on these promises, shut my mouth, and take my eye off my miseries. Then, praying and forgiving those who have angered me will be the lessons that I will achieve through grace, so that I may be restored to the promises of God. Being blessed in my coming and blessed in my going, God will pour out those blessing so large that I can't contain them all and put me back on the path that leads to righteousness, love, justice, peace and prosperity.

Then Job answered the Lord and said:

I know that you can do all things, and that no purpose of yours can be hindered. I have dealt with great things that I do not understand; things too wonderful for me, which I cannot know. I had heard of you by word of mouth, but now my eye has seen you. Therefore I disown what I have said, and repent in dust and ashes.

And it came to pass . . . the Lord said to Job's friends: *I am angry with you and with your two friends for you have not spoken rightly concerning me as has my servant Job.*

And the Lord accepted the intercession of Job.   Also the Lord restored the prosperity of Job, after he had prayed for his friends, the Lord even gave to Job twice as much as he had before.   Thus the Lord blessed the latter days of Job more than his earlier ones.

Job 42

CHAPTER FOUR

SAINTS TO THE RESCUE

This book is long overdue and don't doubt for a moment that I have been under a spiritual attack, for the demons in hell do not want us to know just how big our God is!

I recall the words that St. Therese spoke about her autobiography to Mother Agnes as she was dying. Her poignant request was this:

> "After my death, you must not speak to anyone about my manuscript before it is published; you must speak, only to Mother Prioress about it. If you act otherwise, the devil will lay more than one trap to hinder God's work, a **very important work!**"

> Story of a Soul
> The Spiritual Classic
> of St. Therese of Lisieux

Mother Agnes to whom St. Therese confided those profound concerns about her autobiography was the natural older sister of St. Therese. She was also a Carmelite sister and former prioress at the convent in Lisieux, France, where both sisters resided after taking the veil. Mother Agnes was intimately aware of the special and mystical gifts St. Therese possessed and instructed her to write about her famous *Little Way.*

The autobiography written by St. Therese was later published as *A Story of a Soul* and became one of the most widely read spiritual classics in the world.

I spent many years on a spiritual journey seeking answers to life's many mysteries. I started with an in depth study of the Bible and later moved beyond that to study Lost Books, Apocrypha, various ancient stories and peered into the mysteries contained in the Dead Sea scrolls. The path then led me to study the culture and traditions of various Eastern and Jewish philosophies. It was with abundant joy that I finally stumbled upon the Western mystics that include my patron saint, Therese of Lisieux, as well as St. Teresa of Avila and St. John of the Cross. For me it was like coming home to both my faith and my spiritual experiences.

It seems the Church had their mystics after all, but they were isolated in convents and monasteries. It is with a sense of relief and joy that I embrace the works of these wonderful saints and mystics. Relief in knowing that my beliefs are not heretical and joy in obtaining both the spiritual and religious traditions of the two as they become one!

St. Therese is more to me than my patron saint; she has become my intimate friend and spiritual guide. So, just as St. Therese warned her sister about the manuscript of her own autobiography before her death, I can't help but feel that the devil has laid more than one trap for me since publishing her inspired book and beginning this one about our heavenly Mother.

In just one of the many magical moments that accompanied the process of writing the book inspired by St. Therese, *Communion of Saints*, I recall the events that led up to the selection of the publication date. Like my other books, it was amazingly completed at Christmas and I planned to publish it after the first of the year. I began pondering the date that I should use for publication, sometime in January 2012. The numbers 1-2, 1-2 kept coming to mind and I decided that would be a clever date. As that day approached I had not yet received my proof copy and I awoke that morning wondering if I should put off the publication date until I had time to review it. I considered other dates for publication until I looked on Facebook that morning and found birthday messages everywhere for St. Therese. It was January 2, 2012, (1/2/12) and it was her birthday! That solved my dilemma and answered that question. I immediately went to the website to approve the book for publication and made it official, saying to her in a prayer, *Happy Birthday St. Therese!*

I understood that St. Therese inspired the book I was writing about her and later acknowledged that Mother Agnes was also exercising some spiritual control over that book. I was only the scribe.

I love my saints who help guide me and protect me at all times. The little proofs of their closeness bring such delight and joy.

I have witnessed so many wonderful signs and obtained such great graces from God that it is time for me to start putting all the ingredients together so that my soul may delight in enjoying heaven on earth. I know in my heart that it is possible. I must stay the course and continue by emptying my heart of all the concerns that have plagued me for the past few months and surrender all to my Lord.

So, I begin by declaring:

As an act of faith in the name of Jesus, I surrender my anxieties, anger, frustration, bitterness, resentment, worry and every negative thought, word and deed that has filled my heart. I put all of my love, trust and confidence in You, Lord and I am never disappointed.

I certainly have a lot of trash to unload off my heart. I know that I must empty the concerns and bitterness that have filled it since my injuries morphed into a calamity of traumas that seem to grow exponentially like derailing box cars. I first must unload all of the negative emotions that have accumulated as a result, and then there is more.

As I step out again to untangle myself from these negativities, I have yet another setback. Last week a girl ran a red light and hit my car with such force that it caused eight thousand dollars in damage. It will be in the shop for a month getting repairs. Oh, and did I mention that she said her light was green! My husband just called to tell me his headlights on his truck have stopped working, and on top of that we are looking at the cost of replacing our central heat system that went out last week when it snowed for the first and only time this winter.

I can't seem to catch my breath long enough to compose the prayer, much less empty all this junk in my heart. I am realizing the effect of all this negative energy I am exerting and it is manifesting into horrible circumstances. I know beyond a doubt that I must quickly dispose of it and let God fill my heart with positive energy that will manifest the great things in my life.

My situation is spiraling out of control into a whirlpool of distress. Then there is the stress eating! Ten pounds also need to be dumped along with my negative emotions and thoughts about my calamities!

It is in this seemingly hopeless downward spiral that I recall the words that came to me when God responded to my complaint of anger over my sister's death and the inconsolable grief of my niece.

"YOU DON'T KNOW
HOW I CAN COMFORT HER!"

My God is a comforter! Yes, I need comforting right now, and I am so thankful for my God who is there all the time just waiting for me to cast all my cares and troubles away and fly into those loving arms of protection. Talk about the patience of Job - just imagine the patience of God!

I have much work to do, but I have divine help at hand. With the divine mercy of the Lord, the love and justice of Jesus, the power of God's kindness, the intercession of the saints and the bestowing of God's combined love, grace and comfort, I cannot fail.

I tried surrendering some of this trash just a few days ago. In fact, the day that I let it go was a good day. I received an email from the Chicago Tribune announcing the dates of the next Printers Row Literary Festival. I was anticipating another trip to Chicago where I could premiere the book inspired by my patron saint. I was delighted to get the dates in June so I could plan a return to my home state with Susan. She and I are cousins from Illinois, our mom's being sisters, but we were separated as youngsters when her family moved to California and ours went to Oklahoma.

That evening I went online and reserved rooms in Chicago. Susan had helped publish my book about Mary Magdalene and we had a marvelous time in Chicago last year. In fact, Susan and I have enjoyed many travels together these past years since re-uniting after almost forty years of separation. Susan is my best witness to the help of my saints who have come to our rescue many times during our adventures. My mind filled with happy memories of the outrageous antics we have experienced.

The Miracle Mile hotels were full, as usual, but my heart really desired to go back to Rosemont, Illinois, near O'Hare airport because I loved that Rosemont water tower painted green and covered in red roses. That tower greeted Susan and I on our first trip to Printer's Row. It was so significant of my very favorite saints, Therese of Lisieux and Mary Magdalene. It was both a spectacular welcome and heavenly greeting from my favorite saints to Chicago where we came to premiere, *Trust Me, the Untold Story of Mary Magdalene.*

The roses were symbolic of Therese, the nun known as the Little Flower who is always portrayed in her black habit clutching a crucifix and roses to her breast. The tower was symbolic of Mary Magdalene. Magdalene comes from the word Migdal which means tower.

That tower in Rosemont holds more than just water; it is a beacon of joy for the significant synchronistic blessing it brings to my soul. To me it is a tower of roses symbolic of my special saints, Mary Magdalene and St. Therese of Lisieux.

This year looks to be even more fun. In addition to the premiere of my book inspired by St. Therese, *Communion of* Saints, my niece has written the most fascinating fairytale for children that I hope to publish in time for the Chicago Literary Fest. *Fairies, Sprites and Trolls - a Leprechaun and Moles,* is being illustrated by her daughter and I am so hoping it will all come together by June.

Christy, and her daughter, Lindsay, are both planning to travel with me to Chicago and take their book. My daughter is thinking seriously about joining us in Chicago and Susie wants to return again. Besides all of the family, it will be wonderful to see my girlfriend, Charlene, and her family, too.

Charlene formerly lived in Oklahoma and taught dance to Christy and Michelle when they were young girls, so it would be a super re-union, vacation and business trip all rolled up into one beautiful package and tied with a bow!

Yes, there is light at the end of my tunnel. The same day that I got the email from Printers Row, I also received the note and prayer to Mother Mary from the Benedictine Sisters!

I know something great is about to happen, and I won't let that devil catch me in his traps. My God is too big and too powerful to let me fall into those traps. I am reminded of a favorite biblical verse in Psalms 34 or 35 (depending if the Bible is Catholic of Protestant). This Psalm tells how the Angel of the Lord will drive the enemy down the dark, slippery pathway and let him fall into the pit he dug for me.

February 7, 2012

SURRENDERED & CROWNED. Rosy (my car) is ready at the body shop, one month to the day since the accident, and my dentist placed a crown on my tooth today.

Just a few days ago while praying and surrendering my negative thoughts and feelings, I fell into a state of surrendered bliss. I was having visions of floating on the vast blue ocean of God's love and I truly realized my surrender when I felt the release and relaxing of the muscles occur in the back of my neck just below my skull. Later that day I called my dentist and scheduled the placement of the permanent crown on my troubled tooth. Yes, I knew it was finally time for my crown.

May 15, 2012

My struggles continue with medical treatments by various doctors and denials of claims by insurance lawyers. I have better days than others while I strive to stir up the ingredients for my dessert. I continue to struggle, and at times there are some very low moments.

This day was significant, but certainly not one of my better days. I awoke to the sound of locusts, went outside to find the source of the noise and to my dismay realized it was not outside, but in my ears. To my horror I realized that I was suffering from an incurable disease known as tinnitus. I knew of this disease because I had worked for the medical department in a USAF installation years earlier and had helped process numerous claims for workers stricken with this debilitating disease from exposure to noise.

What I didn't know was that my onset of this frightening disease was yet another car derailing in my series of damaged body parts. Tinnitus is a direct result of the TMJ disorder. I learned this after an appointment with an otolaryngologist who also informed me that it was accompanied by my new high frequency hearing loss. Again there is no treatment or cure for either.

Calling all saints - Help!!

*For the deliberations of mortals are timid,
and unsure are our plans. For the
corruptible body burdens the soul and the
earthen shelter weighs down the mind that
has many concerns. And scarce do we
guess the things on earth, and what is
within our grasp we find with difficulty; but
when things are in heaven, who can search
them out? Or who ever knew your counsel,
except you had given Wisdom and sent
your holy spirit from on high? And thus
were the paths of those on earth made
straight, and men learned what was your
pleasure, and were saved by Wisdom.*

Wisdom 9: 14

CHAPTER FIVE

MIRACLE MILE

June 7, 2012

At last the day has arrived. I am leaving for Chicago! Susan is flying in to meet me at O'Hare Airport to attend the Printers Row Lit Fest. She has been very busy creating a fabulous video to display on the table where the books will be displayed.

We both are so ready for this trip. After all of our adventures in 2009 and 2010 we fell into a slump. The only trip we had managed together in 2011 was a year ago when we came to Chicago for this same event.

"I just can't believe we haven't gone on any trips for a whole year," Susie told me after we found each other.

We met at a restaurant in the terminal and began to catch up on the past year over a drink.

"It's just awful," I sighed. "We just don't have time to waste at our age!"

"We must take another transatlantic cruise this year," I suggested. "You remember the one I emailed you about that goes to Northern France, England and Ireland?" I began. "You might have to skip Paris, so we could go off on another spiritual adventure! You know how much I want to visit the Basilica of St. Therese which is located in northern France," I continued.

Susie just rolled those big green eyes of hers as she remembered me taking her and the priest from the cruise ship in Monte Carlo to travel by car to the Grotto and Basilica of Mary Magdalene. That was quite the adventure. We just made it back to the port in time to jump on the last departing tender returning to our ship. It had been a harrowing experience and one that is chronicled in the *Communion of Saints Inspired by St. Therese*.

Well, here we are back again in Chicago to premier *Communion,* and also display, *Trust Me*, at the Lit Fest on Printer's Row.

It turned out that only Susan and I came to Chicago since my niece's book is not quite ready for this trip.

We also were able to secure a hotel reservation on the Miracle Mile instead of Rosemont which gives us more time to spend in downtown Chicago exploring the famous *Toddlin Town*.

After checking into our room we decided to stay in the hotel for dinner. We both ordered steaks and Susan commented on how much better the steaks are in Illinois than at home.

"It must be the corn fed beef," I suggested.

After dinner Susan took a look at the dessert menu and we were both flabbergasted to find her very favorite and infamous - rhubarb pie!

"Wow." That rhubarb pie must follow you around," I said. "Remember when we started our road trip and you bought a whole rhubarb pie at our first stop in Tulsa? We took that pie with us to St. Louis, Chicago and Decatur and snacked on it with wine every night in our room!"

Naturally, we both ordered the pie and took some of it back to our room. Susan and I had been reminiscing and talking about all the fun we have had on our past trips, along with the amazing synchronicities that only confirmed our saints were with us on our adventures.

"Who introduced you to rhubarb pie?" I asked Susan as we snacked on it later in our room.

"Oh, that was my Aunt Bert who raised me."

I remembered Aunt Bert from childhood visits with Susie when we still lived in Decatur, Illinois. I remember the feather mattress that we slept on and how the feathers would puff up around us as we sunk to the floor on that mattress.

"Well, Susan, Bert is still looking over you for sure." I told her. "Look at these lovely feather duvets on our beds and we are sitting here eating rhubarb pie."

"Oh," Susan replied with surprise, "I never thought of that, but I believe you are right. Bert just adored me when I was a child. I was the daughter she never had and she took care of me. She and Archie were like my parents and I remember how much I loved Archie," she continued.

"In fact I am ashamed that I haven't given Bert more credit than I have."

"Well you know I believe in communion of saints, and I also believe that our loved ones that have passed on are among those saints in heaven who watch over us," I confided in her.

After our snack, Susan pulled out her iPad and began scrolling through her list of things to do in Chicago.

"Now, we have five days to play in Chicago and our first item on the list is to visit the famous Chicago Science Museum. So, that is what we will plan for tomorrow," Susan said taking on her role as the leader just as she always did when we cousins hung out with her younger brother and my younger sister.

Susan was just a few months older than me, but that gave her the leading role in all of our childhood escapades. She still takes the lead role in all of our grownup travels as well, which is fine with me and a very natural position for her. At the same time she is always very flexible in allowing me my spiritual departures which sometimes require saints to the rescue. All in all we have the most enjoyable times when we travel and the most outrageous adventures.

We both had been to the museum as children when we lived in Illinois, so it was way overdue for us to return.

On Friday morning we strolled out onto Michigan Avenue and caught the bus to the museum. We spent hours viewing the amazing displays and stopped to view a movie on the Omnimax screen. We enjoyed looking at trains, airplanes and space exhibits, old town squares and so much more that we lost count. It was a full day and then we took a bus back to our hotel on the Miracle Mile.

Susan is getting to be quite the videographer and she loves her newest electronic gadget that can both record and display her videos. I'm not that savvy and still won't carry a cell phone. I am good on the computer, but that is as far as I have ventured into the field of technology. I think she called the gadget an iPad and then she uses a Kindle to read her books. I being an author, of course, prefer real books!

Susan took videos on the bus ride back, taking in the shores of Lake Michigan, driving by Soldier

Stadium and then of the many skyscrapers that dominate the skyline as we neared our destination.

We had eaten at the museum so we weren't hungry enough to have dinner.

"Martinis and rhubarb pie?" I asked as we headed into the hotel.

"Sure!" Susan responded, as we veered off towards the restaurant.

We brought more of the cherished pie to our room for snacks tonight and breakfast tomorrow.

The next morning was Saturday and time to load up the books and hail a taxi to Printers Row. We were the last ones to arrive at our location in the IWPA tent and we took the last spot left and set up the books and video display.

The first lady to stop by and look at my book with St. Therese on the cover began telling me that the National Shrine of St. Therese was only 30 minutes away.

"Oh my gosh, I didn't know that!" I exclaimed. "I have a girlfriend that lives here and I just know she will take me . . ."

I felt someone step up behind me and turned quickly to see my wonderful friend, Charlene.

"Hi, Charlene, I was just talking about you!" I stuttered, embarrassed.

She gave me a big hug and listened to the lady tell us about the National Shrine of St. Therese that is in Darian, Illinois. Of course, Charlene would take me and Susan to see it tomorrow.

The three of us were getting hungry so we headed over to a coffee shop to get a bite before the show officially opened. Charlene was my best friend in Oklahoma in the 70's and 80's. She was also the best dance teacher in all of Oklahoma. She taught my daughter and niece for years and trained many pageant girls including her own beautiful blonde daughter, Kelly.

It was such a surprise when I found her on Facebook a couple of years ago. How could she be in Chicago when she is from Oklahoma, and I am in Oklahoma and am from Illinois! We had traded places and it was an amazing and a wonderful reunion when Susan and I came to Chicago last year. Now, here we are together again.

"You are going to be a part of our next spiritual adventure!" I told Charlene excitedly.

CHAPTER SIX

SHRINE OF ST. THERESE

June 10, 2012

It's Sunday morning and Susan and I are waiting in our Miracle Mile hotel room to be picked up by Charlene who has generously offered to drive us to the National Shrine of my patron saint and spiritual guide, St. Therese of Lisieux.

Susan is so accommodating to share her trip with me and go on my impromptu excursions. She told me that her girlfriend Susan tells their friends in Sausalito that, "it was a good thing a priest was in the car with them on that wild ride from Monte Carlo to the Grotto of Mary Magdalene, because Susan was ready to kill her cousin!"

They all laugh but it made a great story AFTER we made it back to the ship!

I have the best cousin in Susan and the most wonderful friend in Charlene who both came to my aid to get me to the Shrine of St. Therese. While maneuvering through the Chicago traffic, Charlene told me that her daughter asked if Anne knew how much she loved her to drive into Chicago two times on her weekend off work! I told her I certainly did know that she loved me and I loved her too!

It was a beautiful warm sunny day in June and Charlene could navigate the interstates like a champ. She took us right to the shrine without any difficulty.

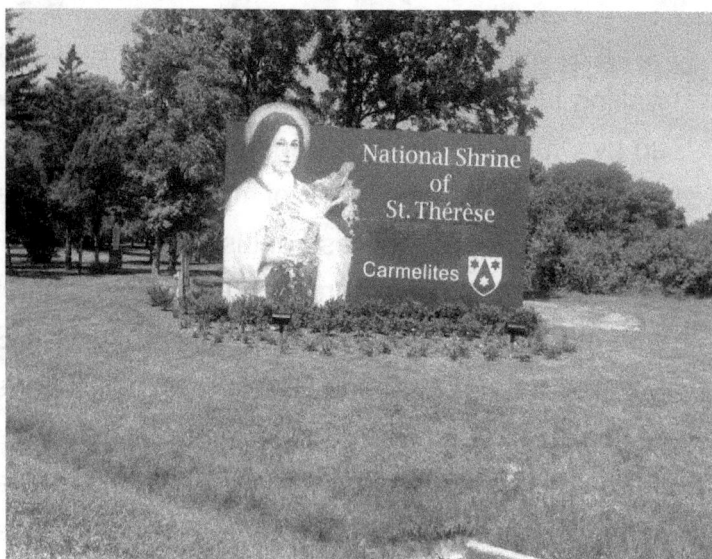

Entrance to the National Shrine of St. Therese

We were all impressed as we drove into the beautiful grounds with grassy knolls, huge shade trees and the brick building that housed the treasures of St. Therese. Just beyond that building was a large white house which I presumed was the convent for the Carmelite sisters that ran this shrine.   There was also a Carmelite Gift Shop adjoining the brick building where we began our visit.

Grounds of the National Shrine of St. Therese

Immediately, upon entering the building I was greeted by the full size statue of St. Therese holding her cross and roses. I knelt and said a short thank you prayer.

Statue of St. Therese inside her National Shrine

I was so happy to be here since I hadn't yet made it to northern France to see the place where she lived and the convent and basilica in her honor.

This shrine contained a myriad of treasures of St. Therese. The most astounding exhibit was the recreated cell of St. Therese where she lived at the convent in France. The window frame, the door and doorway, even tiles in front of the door all came from her actual room in France. I can't explain the excitement that filled my soul as I peered through the glass to see the very room just as it was when she lived in it. I looked and there was the little hourglass on a shelf, along with a little stool that held her writings and pen. The room was very small and very bare as one would expect for this religious.

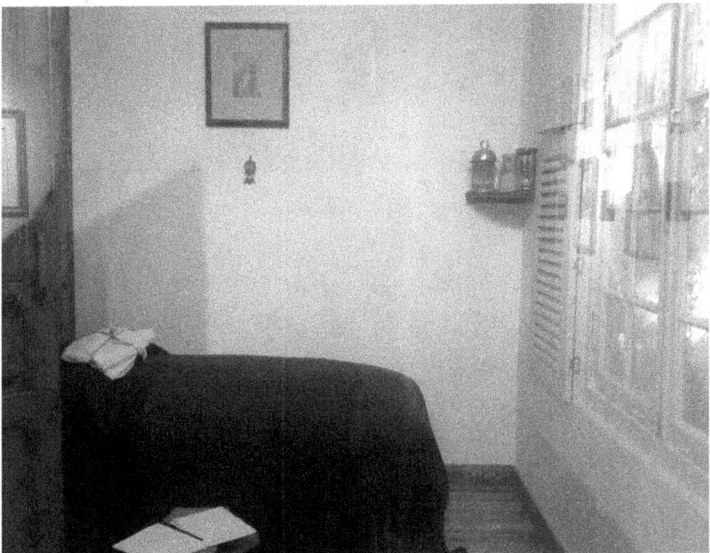

The recreated room of St. Therese

We viewed the sanctuary with stained glass windows and a wall containing a beautiful large wood carved mural depicting the times in the life of St. Therese.

Wooden mural in the sanctuary at the Shrine

My experiences with St. Therese have been more than magical and wondrous. I know her presence and she is my wonderful spiritual guide. To be here in the shrine dedicated to her life was like a dream come true for me. I was in Chicago to premiere her new book, and she brought me to her shrine!

Besides the magic of having her book published on her birthday, I recalled other exciting surprises.

A few days after receiving the proof copy of *Communion of* Saints, I decided to contact the bookstore to schedule my first book signing. The lady on the phone pulled up her calendar and began talking about an available date.

"January is full," she started counting aloud, "and so is February. I can schedule your book signing on March 17th," she told me.

"St. Patrick's Day," I exclaimed. "That is perfect for my book about the saints! I love it, thank you! I will see you then and I will be wearing my green."

After hanging up the phone (yes, I use a land line), I began thinking of all the saints that had helped me with the book and how I had listed their names on the first pages inside the cover. I picked up my book and began reading the names of all the saints. Then, to my horror, I saw that St. Patrick was missing!

How could I have left off the patron saint of Ireland! My mother was full blooded Irish, she went to St. Patrick's school, attended St. Patrick's Church growing up, was even married in St. Patrick's Church on St. Patrick's Day! Oh, this was just awful.

I ran to my computer and brought the book down, added St. Patrick to the page of saints and then put it back up before ordering my copies.

"Well, thank goodness I was able to fix it before the copies were made!"

One would probably think I might be full of the blarney, but this is the truth. I have a shamrock plant in my kitchen window that hasn't had a bloom since I purchased it a year or so ago. The next morning when I went to the kitchen to pour my first cup of coffee, it had sprouted one single white bloom and it was waiting to greet me when I approached the sink!

St. Patrick is appeased and happy!

So many happy thoughts came to my mind while I was touring the National Shrine with Susan and Charlene. Both of them commented on the enormity of the impressions made on them by St. Therese on that short visit. After viewing all of the lovely and beautiful objects in the shrine we then went into the gift shop and browsed.

I couldn't help my next inclination. After all, this was her shrine; the shrine of the saint who had inspired the book. I knew I must leave a copy of it in this place. I approached the ladies at the counter and asked for their book buyer. He was not in the shop, so I left a copy of *Communion of Saints* for his consideration.

We then asked for directions to a nice eating place and left. We enjoyed a nice brunch at a lovely restaurant situated on a nearby local golf course. I never gave any more thought to hearing from anyone about the book, I was just so happy to know that a copy was in her very shrine.

Charlene took us back downtown and we said our goodbyes at the hotel. I thanked Charlene and promised to come back again next year.

Susan and I had one more day to explore Chicago before we headed home on Monday. I always look forward to trips with Susan.

Relics of St. Therese at her Shrine

St. Therese's Bridal Shoes when she
entered the Carmelite Convent at age 15 ½

CHAPTER SEVEN

MOTHER IN HEAVEN

June 21, 2012

Today is the 18th birthday of my great niece, Lauren. My sister Marcia passed away over a decade ago but I know she watches over us along with my Mom in heaven.

I had just attended Lauren's high school graduation last month and was so proud of her. Her mother, Christy, told me that Lauren wanted to be a policeman of all things!

I just couldn't believe it, but I did at the same time. Lauren was all of 5 feet tall, petite with a ton of red curly hair and large blue eyes. She looked like an angel. She was highly intelligent and creative. She could compose and write lyrics, sing and play piano and guitar.

A cop? Really?

She was planning to work while attending a junior college and then move up to a four year college after two years.

I spoke to Christy just last week on the phone and had learned some interesting news.

"My dad has a chance to win a 4 year scholarship at a local university," she told me.

"Wow!" I answered amazed.

"I know," she commented. "I can't believe my dad called into a radio show in the first place. He never calls me and doesn't answer the phone half of the time. But for some unknown reason he called and won a key for a chance to open a vault that contains the scholarship."

"You won't believe this either," she continued, "the date of the vault opening is on Lauren's 18th birthday!"

"Oh my, it just has to be for her." I told Christie. "That certainly is exciting. Your mother in heaven must have had something to do with this. Be sure to keep me posted." I told her as we concluded our call.

Today is Thursday and I missed getting my birthday card in the mail to Lauren in time. I was at the office when I picked up the phone to call Christy to let her know the card was coming as I was going to mail it this morning.

"I've decided to have cake and ice cream for her at the house," Christy told me.

"Great!" I'll bring the card to her party and it will be there right on time."

Then I asked, "Have you talked to your dad? Is he going to the vault opening contest?"

"I don't know," she answered. "You know how my dad never likes to go anywhere. I guess I'll just have to wait and see what happens."

"Okay, I will see you at 7, then," I told her as I hung up the phone.

After work and dinner I changed into some comfortable clothes and headed to Christy's house. She lives about 30 minutes away and I enjoyed some fun music on the radio while I drove out to her place. When I arrived, the house was packed with people; mostly family on her dad's side and lots of friends. There must have been over 30 people that came to this impromptu party.

"Well, you certainly can throw a party together on a moment's notice!" I told my niece.

"Have you heard anything from your dad, yet?" I asked.

"Nope," she replied. "I have been trying to listen to the radio because the contest is being held around 6:30 tonight, but I haven't heard anything," she told me.

Lauren came to the dining room table to open cards and gifts and then blow out candles on her birthday cake after we all sang to her. She was having a great time.

At 8 pm the NBA Finals was being televised and it was game 5 of the 7 series. Oklahoma Thunder was trailing the Miami Heat. This could be the game breaker. I told Christy that I better start heading home so I could get there before dark and watch the game. I hugged her and the kids and drove off.

When I arrived home my phone was ringing and it was Christy. "You just missed my dad!" she told me.

"What? He's there?"

"YES, with the scholarship!" she exclaimed.

I began screaming in the phone and dancing in the living room.

"There were a thousand people there and all those with tickets had a chance for a key," she explained.

"Oh! It was meant to be!" I screamed and jumped up and down I was so excited and happy for Lauren. "Put your dad on the phone, I have to congratulate him!"

"Hello," Johnny answered.

"Johnny, I can't believe it! What a miracle!"

"Yes, it is pretty amazing, I still can't believe it," Johnny told me. "I got one of the five keys and we had to pick a letter in the word 'vault'. So, I picked the letter 'U'."

He continued to explain the process of elimination by telling me, "The first person with the letter 'V' tried his key and he won a computer. I thought to myself I wouldn't mind winning that. Then, the fellow with the letter "A" tried his key and won an iPad. Again, I thought that would be a nice prize."

Johnny was giving me the entire story just as it happened.

"Then, it was my turn," he said. "The letter "U" came up and the radio disc jockey told me to try my key. I told him to wait a minute because first I have to do my happy dance. So, I clowned a bit and the audience clapped. Then, I tried my key and I won the 4-year scholarship!"

"The DJ looked at me and asked what I was going to do with a 4-year college scholarship, and I told him I was taking it to my granddaughter right now. She just graduated from high school and is celebrating her eighteenth birthday with a party tonight! Again the crowd applauded. I was just dumbfounded," he finished.

We chattered for a few more minutes and then he gave the phone back to Christy. She elaborated on the story telling me how he went to the college campus for the contest and there were so many people that he almost left. Then a car pulled out in front of him, so he decided to park and went over to join the crowd. There must have been a thousand people there with tickets that got a chance to try for a key. Somehow they went through people until they found the 5 keys to the vault. Johnny already had one of them.

Christy then explained how her dad drove up to her house in his Corvette and Lauren was playing with some of the kids outside. Then, he walked over to her with the college logo bag on his shoulder and when she saw it she started to cry. Christy went outside and she too began to cry. Then, one of the girls there started taking pictures and she began to cry.

I was so disappointed that I had missed it all, but I was too happy to be very disappointed. She told me I had just missed Johnny by a few minutes.

It was such a happy day that even the Thunder loss to Miami couldn't dampen my spirits. The

Thunder did a wonderful job winning the Western Division and going 5 games in the National championship. Oklahoma was very proud of their young new team. Only four years in Oklahoma City and we had the Western Division Champs who really gave Miami a run for their title.

I spoke to Christy again the next day and learned that Johnny and Lauren would be going to the university to have pictures made soon. We couldn't help but believe that her mother, Johnny's wife, my sister, and Lauren's Grandmother Marcia had a hand in this wonderful gift that came to Lauren like a blessing from heaven. We surely know our loved ones are watching over us from above; and that my Mom and Marcia are so happy to be in heaven together. We are also very happy that we can feel their love and presence around us.

Christy told me another fascinating aspect to the scholarship. Someone at the party asked Lauren if that school would have the criminology courses that she was interested in studying. And, another person told her that the university had just added on a forensic science lab that was state of the art. This brought on even more tears as Lauren enjoyed that very special night of her 18th birthday.

CHAPTER EIGHT
ANOTHER VISIT

Sunday, July 22, 2012

It is a scorching hot Sunday in Oklahoma. The temperatures have been triple digit all week and today promises to reach 109 degrees. My daughter has been on a mission to update her salon this weekend. She has tons of expensive fabric to make drapes for the large front windows and her Dallas girlfriend can sew. Susan generously offered to come to Oklahoma City to make Michelle's drapes and drove up on Friday night bringing her sewing machine. The girls have been busy bees for the past two days.

Michelle is especially excited about the drapes coming together at last, because she purchased the material over a year ago. Susan has been working furiously for two days to complete the beautiful new draperies for Michelle's salon.

Of course, the drapes match wonder dog Daisy, Michelle's silvery taupe Weimaraner. I believe Michelle matches everything to that dog's color. She sent me a photo of Daisy and the new drapes.

Yes, a perfect match!

Daisy and the curtains

Magic began happening yesterday with the sewing marathon. I stopped by my daughter's house to see the material and then left the girls to their tasks while I ran my usual weekend errands. After picking up groceries, my next stop was at the nearby hardware store. My inner voice was directing my attention to the Tuesday Morning store a few doors down and a parking place right in front invited me to come in.

As I browsed the first aisle I came upon a group of curtain rods. Well, I had to check that out since the girls would need rods before they could hang the new drapes. I took out a pen and scribbled a short note with the measurements and styles available and headed home.

After putting the groceries away, I called Michelle to tell her about the rods I had found and began describing them to her. As soon as I got past the pewter and black and described the chrome with crystal ball finials she gasped. I knew I had found the right ones.

Later, Michelle called. "You are fabulous!" she told me. "The rods are exactly what I needed; and even better than that I found the perfect material to line my drapes."

This morning Michelle called to tell me Susan had spent another night in order to finish the project.

"We are on our way to the salon to hang the new drapes, if you want to come and watch," she told me.

"Oh, I will be right over!" I said excitedly. Being a part of Michelle's project was exhilarating. She exudes an enthusiasm that is contagious, inspiring joy in all those around her.

When I arrived I found Michelle on a ladder with her drill and hammer installing the rod holders. Susan showed me the tons of material that was stacked and draped over the sofa that were the new coveted drapes.

"These are so heavy," Susan explained, "that I can only carry two panels at a time. We made eight panels and lined all of them."

As Susan showed me the beautiful drapes, Michelle explained the process that took place.

"When we went to look at the curtain rods, we also needed to find material to line the drapes. We had planned to go to the fabric stores, but I told Susan we should look around this store further. Then, we found these drapes that had the blackout lining needed to block my west sun, and the color and measurements were absolutely perfect." Michelle continued.

"They were so beautiful that had I found these a year ago I would have bought them instead of trying to have drapes made. So, I bought the drapes, took them home and decided to attach them to the new drapes. I told Susan we should turn the beautiful side to the outside and she agreed. That is how they have been sewn together, and now they are beautiful from both sides and totally perfect," she finished.

At last the time arrived and the curtains were strung along the rods.

"Spectacular!" I gasped.

We all stepped back to admire the gorgeous new window, then went outside and that view was incredible. Each panel was topped with delicate and beautiful folds that were regal and captivating.

Magic had truly happened in the making of these drapes. They totally changed the dynamic of the salon inside and out. The drapes effected an elegance while their essence was captivating and inviting.

They just spoke to the soul saying, *Welcome. Come and stay awhile.*

It was a moment of celebration as we all hugged and enjoyed being a part of this exciting finale. Michelle decided she wanted to re-arrange the furniture and Susan was ready to head home to Dallas.

I stayed and helped Michelle as she transformed the salon. I traveled with her to pick up more pictures, plants and other items for the final touches.

We were still very excited about the great transformation and how marvelously the universe had performed synchronistic magic to make everything come together perfectly.

It was such a happy day. While running errands in the car I began telling Michelle about my own special gift that had been imparted to me today.

"This morning I took time to read the card I had recently received form the Missionary Oblates of Mary Immaculate and it told the story of Our Lady of Lourdes."

Michelle drove and I continued to tell her about my thoughts on Mary.

"I knew that Lourdes was in France, but today this story conveyed a special meaning to me when I read that Lourdes was located in s*outhwestern France.* You remember I made two trips to *southern France* when I visited the grotto and basilica of Mary Magdalene."

"Meanwhile," I continued, "I have been procrastinating on writing my book about the Mother of God and I just knew this information was a gift. I am curious to see just where Lourdes is located on a map, and how far it is from that grotto and basilica."

Well, time was running short because Michelle had plans to meet several girlfriends for lunch and a movie. We rushed in and out of stores, her house and back to the salon where she put the finishing touches on the place. She hung pictures, potted plants that she placed on either side of the entrance and put out a new door mat.

We stood back to admire the entrance and I walked across the parking lot toward the street and insisted that Michelle come out and see the view from there. It was at that moment a girl approached on the sidewalk and asked if we could tell her how far it was to Memorial. She was pale, fragile and getting sunburned. We knew it was at least another 5 miles from the salon to her destination - and Michelle looked panicked because the time for her to meet her friends was bearing down too fast for any more delays.

Michelle also knew it was way too hot for this girl to walk that far and looked toward me. So, I motioned to the girl and said "Get into my car, I can take you there."

My time was tight as well since I had a roast waiting to come out of the oven, a hungry husband waiting for dinner, and I, too, was planning to catch up with the girls at the restaurant and join them for the movie.

"My name is Anne," I said to my guest as I pulled out onto the street. She told me her name and our conversation began as we drove toward her destination.

I looked at her big blue eyes and fair skin that was turning pink, and said to her, "You must be Irish with that fair skin."

"Yes, I am," she replied.

"I thought so."

She had explained to us on the sidewalk that she was stranded because her purse and ID had been stolen and she was going to a certain place where she could pick up a money transfer from her son without an ID.

"You should ask St. Anthony to help you find your purse," I continued. "My full blooded Irish Catholic mom always called on St. Anthony every time she lost anything. He is the patron saint of lost things and he will help you find it."

"Oh, then I bet your mother was very superstitious," she answered as she began describing different superstitions of the Irish.

"Of course, and to this day I won't ever kill a cricket because it is bad luck," I laughed.

"Michelle is my daughter and she owns the salon where we were hanging new drapes and putting out new potted plants to spruce the place up," I told my passenger. "Michelle is a master colorist, one of only a few in the state and I am so proud of her," I remarked.

"Do you have children?" I asked.

She began describing two sons on different coasts in their twenties. That was when I realized she was probably Michelle's age.

I told her I had a grandson that just turned 26, and I was about to become a great-grandmother in September.

"Don't you feel lucky?" she asked. "You look so good, I mean really good."

"Oh, thank you!" I laughed. Then told her to name her place - I would take her anywhere.

By now we were nearing her destination and I showed her the mall that was near and told her there were some hotels in the area.

"Are you sure you will be alright?" I asked before she departed.

"Yes, yes," she said confidently. "My son has been on the internet and checking hotels where I can stay until he can get my birth certificate to me so I will be able to get on a plane." "Thank you so very much for bringing me here," she said.

And, then she stepped out of the car and I raced to get home before the roast burned up.

As I headed home I realized that her appearance was so very similar to my visit a few years ago by Therese and Maggie. These two young ladies had stepped out to speak to me on the sidewalk downtown as I walked to my office. They too had been stranded here until Travelers Aide could arrange their travel.

As related in *Communion* these special visitors turned out to be none other than my favorite saints, Therese and Mary Magdalene - and St. Therese hugged me!

Oh, my. I have again been visited by a saint. I thought to myself. *Which one? I can't remember the name she told me!*

I thought maybe Maggie had visited again. I have been praying about my new book *The Mother Who Loves You,* just as I prayed and asked for answers about Mary Magdalene when I wrote about her in *Trust Me.*

I have been praying to Mother Mary and the saints, and I know this visit is directly related to my new book. I am excited and ready to continue writing.

"Thank you, Maggie - Thank you, Mother."

Or was it Mother? Could it be? I anxiously await the confirmation of my visitor's identity. Funny - she didn't have her ID.

When I caught up with Michelle and we had a moment to talk, she told me how bad she felt for that girl. She could tell she had cancer.

"Really, how did you know that she had cancer?" I asked Michelle.

"She was wearing a turban and she had no hair, lashes or eyebrows. She had obviously had chemotherapy," Michelle informed me.

"Oh I never even noticed," I replied. "All I could see were her beautiful blue eyes and fair skin. But, now that you mention it, she did tell me she had just finished chemotherapy."

I recalled more of our conversation on the short drive and told Michelle what I could remember.

"She talked about two sons and told me she had come here to watch a niece compete in the American Idol competitions, but she had not been selected."

"Then, I told her about my niece's daughter who was so gifted musically, but she hadn't wanted to compete this year because she was concentrating on starting college."

"The lady said that it was good to put your education ahead of your dreams, but stressed that you should not give up your dreams, just keep things in perspective."

"She also lamented that one son had tattoos and even worse than the tattoos was something he wore in his ear and she pointed to her right ear."

I recalled more of our conversation as I asked if they were those multi-piercings.

"No, much worse than that," she told me. "He puts something in his ear that stretches it and makes it larger."

"Oh, no," I gasped, "that sounds horrible!"

She then proceeded to say that reverse psychology still worked even though her son was grown. After protesting to no avail she gave up on that, and told him she was beginning to like it.

"Then he stopped doing it," she said.

I confided in Michelle how I knew this stranger showing up was something special. It was too similar to the way I met Maggie and Therese on a sidewalk and they were also stranded here for a day or more. Michelle agreed that she knew the lady was meant for me to take and not her.

So, now I wait for more pieces of this story to be revealed - - and I am getting excited about this book and the story that is about to unfold.

After lying down for the night, I said a short thank you prayer to Mother Mary and wondered again about my conversation at the point when I told my guest my name.   And then just like a bolt, I remembered the name she gave me.

Reba, I remembered! *My thoughts were jubilant.*

CHAPTER NINE

REBECCA

For days and weeks after my encounter with Reba I continued to wonder about the meaning of her visit. I recalled more of our conversation and was determined to understand the messages conveyed to me while I was in her presence.

An Internet search turned up information about the name Reba that was very interesting. First, I learned that Reba is an ancient Hebrew name meaning *to bind* and comes from the original word *Rivka*. Rivka is also associated with managing livestock, hence meaning *manger* and *cord*. The name Reba is a derivative of the biblical name Rebecca.

Now I have found a biblical reference for my deeper scriptural study. This is exciting because this story is beginning to unfold so much like the story of Mary Magdalene did as I wrote her story in *Trust Me*. I can remember wondering where to begin my search for answers to the puzzling story of Mary Magdalene. I began with a prayer to her and immediately two biblical books were conveyed to me. Those were the Book of Ruth and the Canticle of Canticles.

In attempting to write this story about the Mother Who Loves You, I have followed the same pattern. I have been in prayer to Mother Mary to bring me the story. That is why I am so confident that the visit form the lady was an answer to that prayer. In patience and prayer I will continue to seek her story.

I now know and understand that the lady I met who was stranded in Oklahoma City without any identification was none other than my Mother in Heaven!

In the Book of Genesis I read the story of Rebecca. She was the bride that Abraham sought to find for his son Isaac before he passed away. He called his servant and adjured him not to obtain a wife for his son among the Canaanites where he lived, but to go back to his land and kindred to find a wife for his son.

As the story goes this servant was given treasures and camels and sent on his way. He prayed to the Lord to grant him success on his journey. The servant found a young woman and she took him to her father's house. Her father was the brother of Abraham and thus she was the niece of Abraham.

This follows interestingly with the information I obtained from Reba in that she was here to see her niece compete in the American Idol tryouts. The niece is a clue about the lady that I met. It is one of those significant coincidences in that Rebecca is described as the niece of Abraham.

Rebecca agreed to go with the servant and become the bride of Isaac and when Isaac saw her approaching he took her to wife and it is written that he loved her and was consoled for the loss of his mother.

Isaac was forty years old when they married and he prayed to the Lord for she was barren and the Lord answered his prayer and Rebecca conceived. The children jostled each other within her womb and she consulted the Lord and asked,

"If this be so, why am I pregnant?' He said to her, "Two nations are in your womb; two peoples shall stem from your body. One people shall be stronger than the other, and the elder shall serve the younger."

> *When the time came she indeed bore twins. The first to come forth was red. His whole body was like a hairy garment, and so they named him Esau. Afterwards his brother came forth, with his hand gripping Esau's heel; so he was called Jacob. Isaac was sixty years old when they were born.*

Genesis 25:24-26

> *When the boys grew up, Esau became a skillful hunter, a man of the open country, while Jacob was a settled man who stayed among the tents. Isaac preferred Esau because he was fond of the game, but Rebecca preferred Jacob.*

Genesis 25:27-28

This particular story in the Bible has always intrigued me. It seemed to be a similitude of the very story of Adam and Eve who also had two sons, one red and hairy that they named Cain and his brother, Abel. We know in this instance that Cain went away to the east of Eden after slaying his brother. Two nations effectively came into the world as it became populated by Cain's descendants in one place and the descendants of Adam through Seth in another. Just like Esau and Isaac, Cain also lost his standing as first born to Abel the younger son who obeyed God.

In the Lost Books of Eden the story unfolded that Cain and Abel were each born with a twin sister. After Cain murdered his brother and went away the book tells how the descendants of Adam remained on the mountain and served God, while the descendants of Cain behaved sinfully below and would try to lure the good children down. Those that ventured down the mountain were never able to return to their home.

I have written about the conclusions that I formed from my intense study of the Scriptures, Apocrypha and ancient scrolls and stories that have come to light. My most astonishing conclusion was my belief that Abel returned to the earth as Jesus.

While writing the story of Mary Magdalene I was directed to the story of Ruth which so reminded me of the story of Eve and her two daughters that had been married to her sons. Ruth had lost her sons and husband and the one daughter remained with her. Similarly, Eve outlived Adam and Abel. Both Eve and Ruth were widows who lost sons, and the daughters remained. The entire story unfolds in my book, *Trust Me.*

Getting back to Rebecca, the Jewish scriptures describe her as a character known for her beauty and cunning. Abraham, the Patriarch of the Jews, obtains her hand for his son Isaac. She is embroiled in the conflict between her twin boys, Esau and Jacob, and encourages Jacob (her favorite) to deceive his father and steal his brother's birthright.

Esau was the stronger and as told to Rebecca the elder served the younger, Jacob. They parted from each other to live in different places.

With this in mind, I began recalling the stories that Reba had told me about her own sons. It seemed one lived on the east coast, probably New York, for she told me this son doesn't have a driver's license. He is concerned with the earth and not driving cars that pollute. She confided to me that she had a BMW convertible and her son chided her about the pollution. But she told him he made up for it since he didn't drive. She also told me she had never ridden on a bus.

The remark about the bus brought back my memory of meeting Maggie and Therese across from the bus station just 10 days before my first trip to Mary Magdalene's basilica in October of 2009. This stirs my excitement and expectation of something great being about to happen.

I wondered if I would finally get word if I was accepted to attend the book fest in Boston which will be held in October. My mind is filling with all kinds of wonderful scenarios and great expectations.

The name given me by my beautiful visitor was significant in bringing the story of Rebecca to my attention; and her story bears witness to the ancient story of the birth of twins and two nations where the elder served the younger.

Reba also emphasized an important message when she described her son that wore the ear stretcher in his ear. I believe she was conveying to us that the devil has a big ear that is always listening to our words. We know that the devil has no power of his own and that is why he lures us into speaking wrong words against ourselves. For our words have power and that is the only way he can trap us. She was showing us that we should ignore the annoying distractions rather than focusing on them, then the devil quits using them because he is not as clever as he pretends.

Statue of Mary, the Immaculate Conception

CHAPTER TEN

ENLIGHTENMENT

I am encouraged by the Lord and so thankful that my saints are still showing up for this book, just as they did for the book I wrote about them. Blessed encouragement!

I recall the date of my first book signing for *Trust Me* being on 5/21/2011. This was significant since the Lord had spoken the words to me so many years ago when I awoke and heard the question, "What are your initials?"

"A-C-T," I answered.

"5-2-1," the voice responded.

As I came fully awake I repeated, "ACT 521." "*What could that mean?*" I wondered.

I picked up my favorite well-worn Bible and looked up the Book of Acts, Chapter 5; Verse 21:

Go, stand, and speak in the temple
all the words of this life.

I retell this story because the numbers 5-2-1 became very special to me, and I was absolutely thrilled when I realized that the date for the signing of my very first officially published book, *Trust Me,* was scheduled on May 21st or 5-2-1!

You can imagine my delight again to have my first book signing for *Communion of Saints Inspired by St. Therese* scheduled on March 17th - St. Patrick's Day! Of course, the saints' book would premiere on a blessed saint's day - and an Irish saint at that, who is celebrated every year!

I let my mind wander randomly as I enthuse over the many wonders that I have experienced on my spiritual journey. I let those thoughts penetrate my mind like a light soaking rain as I continue to write this most difficult of all books about the Mother of God.

I just learned that my significant visit from the beautiful lady occurred on the Feast Day of Mary Magdalene, July 22nd. At the same time I found that January 1st is the Feast Day of Mary, the Mother of God.

This is a significant revelation to me since I have struggled so with this book and actually went past the Christmas Day finish that occurred magically for the completion of my other books. As I continue to organize my notes and chapters I have to wonder if this book will magically be completed on January 1st, her feast day. It would certainly take a miracle for that to happen, since today is December 30th and I am going out of town tomorrow to celebrate New Year's Eve again with my wonderful husband who always takes me dancing on that special night.

Returning to my thoughts I am reminded of the extreme importance of the Commandment to *Honor Your Mother and Your Father*. This Commandment comes with a promise that you will live long and well in the land. You honor your heavenly Mother and Father when you honor your earthly parents.

I learned this lesson the hard way when I fiercely opposed my own mother many years ago. She wisely told me that the man I was dating was no good. To my dismay I realized too late how right she was. By then I was trapped in a marriage with a sociopath and spent years in desolation and hopelessness until I found my miraculous escape from the darkest pit to the pinnacle of light.

Fortunately, my gracious and long suffering mother forgave me and we became even more closely connected following those years of torment.

In an abrupt departure from this story comes a poignant insistent thought that I must address at this juncture. It is easier to gloss over the six years I suffered during my marriage to a sociopath than to relive and discuss the details openly. However, I do believe it impacts this story and more importantly sheds light on the peculiar defense mechanisms that are sparked by emotional captivity.

Yes, being trapped with a sociopath or psychopath is very similar to being held by a terrorist. Survival instincts fire rapidly in response to each emotionally debilitating circumstance. The responses are not thought through sensibly because they are manifested instantly in response to terrorizing threats, both emotional and physical.

It was in the midst of horrendous fear, helplessness and hopelessness instilled by this psychopath that the natural instinct to protect my beautiful young daughter misfired into protective mode. Not knowing what to do and having no place to turn, I did the only the thing I could to protect her. I explained to her that we must not show our deep affection around this man because his jealousy was so extreme. We had to literally close up and hide our true feelings for each other in an effort to protect ourselves from danger. Hiding our love was the most excruciatingly painful emotion that I ever suffered. My fierce love for my daughter and the overwhelming need to protect her resulted in her leaving home when she was fourteen. She shuffled between relatives and friends because she knew she could not stay with me because her presence placed us both in danger.

These protective measures caused emotional blockages that affected both of us for years after our escape from these self-imposed and invisible prisons.

My shame could not be abated for abandoning my little girl. But one day many years later came an awakening and recognition of the fact that I was not completely guilty of blatant abandonment. A story hit the headline news and it also hit home.

The most interesting and puzzling story unfolded right here in Oklahoma when a prison guard's wife was caught living with an escaped prisoner somewhere in the South on a chicken farm. They had disappeared many years ago from the prison grounds where she lived with her husband and daughters.

The tabloids were having a heyday with stories of how she had abandoned her family to help this man escape. No one could understand how she could do that. Her condemnation was the same that I had been suffering silently by my own guilty feelings. There was no logical or understandable excuse for her actions. But, when she told authorities that her children were in danger of this psychopath if she ever left him - I knew exactly what she was saying!

This is when the discussion arose about Stockholm Syndrome, also called capture-bonding. It is described as a psychological phenomenon in which hostages express empathy, sympathy and have positive feelings towards their captors. What a revelation this was for me to learn there was a name and a diagnosis for my behavior. My actions are medically defined! I am not wholly to blame for everything that happened because I was suffering from this very syndrome. It was an emotionally charged realization that set me free from my long lived tortuous guilt.

I empathized with this woman and followed her story as she was ridiculed and slandered in the public arena of judgment. I had even worked for her attorney briefly in my years of doing temp work so my interest in the outcome was twofold.

She endured a trial that lasted for months, but in the end she was judged guilty of helping the man escape from prison. It seemed that I was the only one who understood her plight. My take on the whole spectacle was much different than that of the jurors. To this day I believe that justice was maligned. The blame should have been placed properly on the prison officials who allowed a murdering psychopath to roam freely on the grounds preying on and capturing an innocent victim. And, rather than serving time in jail, this woman and her family should have been compensated for years of suffering, separation and loss that were caused by the very institution that brought charges against her - - the state.

The men in charge of that prison were the dupes who allowed this con artist to have free run of the very place where he was supposed to be confined. The guard's wife was victimized by both her captor and those charged with protecting her and our society from a convicted psychopathic murderer who should have rightfully been kept behind bars.

These long winding stories revolve around one important subject and that is captivity. In a diabolical twist the captive becomes the guilty party - not the captor.

I believe a light is shining from heaven on the thousands of women who have suffered emotional and physical abuse at the hands of their captors. The sin of captivity is as old as the sin of murder. Both took place at the very beginning with the first family to inhabit the earth.

I am not surprised that this story unwittingly surfaced from deep within my soul and spewed out over these pages; for it is a fitting and poignant demonstration of the demonic devices that were put into play from the beginning of time in an attempt to destroy the children of God. Murder and captivity are two of the chief tools used by Satan or Beliar, as he is called in the Lost Books.

According to the story of Adam and Eve as related in the Forgotten Books of Eden, the first children conceived in heaven and born into the earth were Cain with a twin sister, Luluwa; and Abel with his twin sister, Aklia. Later, Adam and Eve planned to have Abel marry Luluwa, the beautiful red haired twin sister of Cain. The devil then came to Cain and taunted him saying that his brother was the favored child and provoked him into a jealous rage. Jealousy was the motive that drove Cain to murder Abel and then he took Luluwa captive.

Murky shades of grey are barely discernible between the worlds of brilliant light and darkest black; and that old serpent continues to scheme in his determination to deter us from the blissful rainbow of light so he can take us down with him to the miserable blackest pit of hell.

It is important to emphasize that Luluwa was the feminine spiritual being created in God's image along with Abel the masculine spiritual being for the union which brought about the salvation of fallen mankind. Why then am I not surprised that when Luluwa was returned to earth as Mary Magdalene to be reunited with Abel as Jesus for the victorious marriage feast, that she was later publicly humiliated, denounced and declared a prostitute!

It is time to draw back the veil that has hidden the feminine spirit of God since the beginning of time when God created man in his image - male and female. The victory could not be won by man alone - it took two to become one; and therein the age old mystery of the Bible is solved that declares:

> The Lord God cast the man into a deep sleep and while he slept, took one of his ribs and closed up its place with flesh. And the rib which the Lord God took from the man, he made into a woman and brought her to him. Then the man said, "She now is bone of my bone, and flesh of my flesh; she shall be called Woman, for from man she has been taken." For this reason a man leaves his father and mother, and clings to his wife, and the two become one flesh.
> Genesis 2:24

I can say that out of my struggle and pain I obtained mercy that brought me to new heights in spiritual understanding. God never forsakes us, and when we learn to forgive and put our trust in God; He and She is more than pleased to restore and bless us abundantly. Welcoming us home like lost children, we obtain amazing transformation that turns our guilt into innocence; our sorrow into joy; and our misery into happiness. I have found that resting in God's arms is the only place to dwell.

Continuing in the path of my thoughts, I am lead to a scripture about the wedding feast.

> *The kingdom of heaven is like a king who made a marriage feast for his son. And he sent his servants to call in those invited to the marriage feast, but they would not come. . . .*

> *But when the king heard of it, he was angry . . . saying the marriage feast is indeed ready, but those who were invited were not worthy.*

> Matthew 22; 3-9

This verse reiterates my belief that Jesus and Mary Magdalene were wed and that Mother Mary was present - - at the wedding feast in Cana where Jesus performed his first miracle by turning the water into wine. This miracle is significant in describing their mystical union as the two are changed from the ordinary (water) into the extraordinary (wine).

This union completed the ancient mystery that took place after Adam and Eve were turned out of the Garden. We have not been told or made aware of the feminine aspect of this incredible feat, but it was through this union of the male and female - the very image of God, that we have all become reunited with God and are now called children of God.

The explanation of physical realities that are born beneath the surface of our mind and created in the soul is about to unfold on these blank pages. This book is about our thoughts and the effect they have on the manifestation of good and evil. And, I believe that in order to better understand our complex structure which is a combination of spiritual and physical components, it is necessary to return to the very first family of Adam and Eve.

While pondering how I can explain the story of creation as I have come to understand it, I realize the enormity of the task and am prompted to create a family tree in order to better describe the complexities of the first family, who are both heavenly and earthly beings.

The Original Family Tree

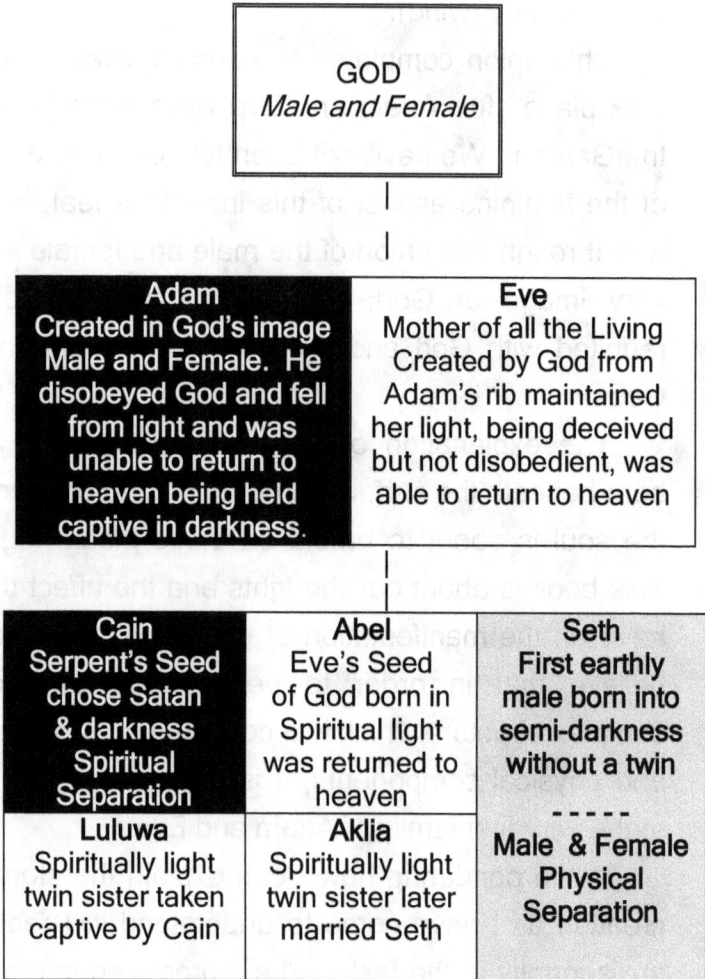

GOD
Male and Female

Adam	Eve
Created in God's image Male and Female. He disobeyed God and fell from light and was unable to return to heaven being held captive in darkness.	Mother of all the Living Created by God from Adam's rib maintained her light, being deceived but not disobedient, was able to return to heaven

Cain	Abel	Seth
Serpent's Seed chose Satan & darkness Spiritual Separation	Eve's Seed of God born in Spiritual light was returned to heaven	First earthly male born into semi-darkness without a twin
Luluwa Spiritually light twin sister taken captive by Cain	**Aklia** Spiritually light twin sister later married Seth	- - - - - Male & Female Physical Separation

Note the position of the children that could bring about the restoration of mankind in God's image,

male and female, containing the heavenly light or
Spirit of God.

The first children of Eve were spiritually
conceived in the light of heaven. Even though Cain
was spiritually conceived by a lie, he had a choice
between light and darkness.

> *The Lord said to Cain, "Why are you angry*
> *and why are you downcast? If you do well,*
> *will you not be accepted; but if you do not*
> *do well, will not sin crouch at the door! Its*
> *desire is for you, but you must master it."*
>
> *Genesis 4: 6-7*

Cain ignored God's words and chose to follow
Satan. He murdered his brother and took Luluwa
captive. Cain's soul entered into spiritual darkness,
but the other three children remained in the spiritual
light of God.

It seems clear from this diagram that Adam and
Eve would plan the marriage of Abel to Luluwa
since they were born of different seeds. The death
of Abel and capture of Luluwa seemed to forever
preclude this intended union.

Later, Adam and Eve conceived a son in the
earth. Seth was born into a physical semi-dark
nature and married Aklia with the spiritual light
nature. The descendants of Adam are described in

the Bible beginning with Seth. These children stemmed from the dark-light union of Seth and Aklia.

Meanwhile, Cain who chose the darkness and married Luluwa the other spiritually light soul, brought forth descendants stemming from a similar dark-light union. The Bible describes these descendants as the children of Cain, *who knew his wife.*

This clearly demonstrates that both lineages had a mixture of light and dark; spiritual and physical qualities. We truly do have a choice between light and darkness. Our physical body dies then our spiritual nature lives for eternity. Our choice determines if that eternity is in darkness or in light, in heaven with God or in hell forever banished from our Father and Mother.

All knowing and almighty God saved Adam by the children conceived by Eve in heaven when she brought forth the twins in the earth. A remnant of each seed born of the light and the only two who could possibly accomplish the feat of male and female spiritual union were Abel and Luluwa.

What appeared in the flesh to be impossible when Abel was murdered and Luluwa was taken captive was spiritually possible for God. The remaining spiritual creatures of light, Eve, Abel and Luluwa, were brought back to heaven by God when they completed their earthly lives. The devil was not able to keep them captive in the earth. You might remember the biblical stories which describe the devil pursuing the woman who is about to give birth so that he might devour her offspring.

There was a time prescribed by God for Adam to be brought back into heaven. In the Lost Books God told Adam that he would return in the flesh and bring him back to heaven after 5 ½ days, further explaining that a day in heaven is like a thousand years in the earth.

In keeping with that promise, God returns the three spiritual beings to earth in the flesh as Mary, Jesus and Mary Magdalene; the same spiritual beings that formerly lived in the earth as Eve, Abel and Luluwa.

The marriage at Cana was the culmination of God's plan to restore mankind to the kingdom of heaven. This marriage feast recreated the original creation of God, male and female, Adam and Eve. Mary Magdalene, the daughter incarnate of Mother God, Eve, is joined to Jesus, the Son of Father God incarnate, and they become one flesh!

Christians everywhere believe the salvation story that Jesus overcame sin, died in the flesh and was taken to heaven. I would elaborate on this story to include the female in accomplishing the sacred union that would bring about the complete and whole restoration of all God's children.

The Lost Books give greater detail of the victory after Jesus died. It tells how Jesus entered the dark pit in all of his majesty, power and light. The devils shook with fear when He appeared in all of his majesty. Then, Jesus brought all the souls up out of captivity - beginning with his father, Adam!

I love the detail that I found like hidden treasures contained in The Lost Books of the Bible and Forgotten Books of Eden.

The union of Jesus and Mary Magdalene is such a remarkably magnificent accomplishment of salvation that it is no wonder the Bible says God was angry when we failed to attend His *Marriage Feast!*

The Canticle of Canticles

Bridegroom: Open to me, my sister, my beloved,
my dove, my perfect one!
Bride: I took hold of him and would not let him go
till I should bring him to the home of my mother,
to the room of my parent.
I adjure you, daughters of Jerusalem . . . do not arouse,
do not stir up love before its own time.
Bridegroom: I have come to my bride;
I gather my myrrh and my spices.
Bride: I was sleeping, but my heart kept vigil;
I heard my lover knocking.
Bridegroom: One alone is my dove, my perfect one,
her mother's chosen, the dear one of her parent.
Bride: Oh, that you were my brother,
nursed at my mother's breasts!
If I met you out of doors,
I would kiss you and none would taunt me.
I would lead you, bring you into the home of my mother.
Bridegroom: Under the apple tree I awakened you;
it was there that your mother conceived you.
It was there that your parent conceived.
You are an enclosed garden,
My Sister, My Bride.

This is enlightenment.

The Pieta
Mother Mary and her children

*Located at the entrance to Mary Magdalene's Grotto
in Sainte-Baume, Aix-en-Provence, France*

Stairs atop mountain leading to Mary Magdalene's Grotto

CHAPTER ELEVEN
THE MESSAGE

I have been researching material on appearances of Mother Mary because I have come to know that it was She, Herself, who visited me on that significant 22nd day in July, 2012, on the very Feast Day of Mary Magdalene.

In a book entitled, *Miracles of Mary*, by Michael Durham, I found the wonderful stories of the many visitations of Mary from the 1st century to the present, and I refer to this book for the facts of the following stories about the Holy Mother.

First, I was honored to have the opportunity to visit her most famous shrine in Fatima a couple of years ago when Susan and I took a luxurious transatlantic cruise to the Mediterranean. One of the excursions we selected was to visit Fatima in Portugal.

This shrine commemorates the repeated visits of Mary to three children in a village in Portugal. It is now a beautiful and massive memorial to Mary where millions of faithful come to visit annually.

The story of her visit to the children at Fatima is especially poignant as The Lady conveyed mysteries and prophecies to Lucia, one of the three children who later became a Carmelite nun in 1948. It is recorded that Mary appeared on six occasions to the children from May 13 through October 13, 1917. On her third apparition on July 13, 1917, Mary imparted three secrets to the children and the third secret was never revealed.

The first secret was the vision of Hell and The Lady telling the children that God is going to punish the world for its crimes by means of war, hunger and persecution of the Church and the Holy Father.

The second secret was about the consecration of Russia to her Immaculate Heart when the lady explained if Russia listened and be converted there would be peace, if not Russia would provoke wars and persecution of the Church. She told them in the end her Immaculate Heart would triumph.

The third secret has never been revealed. Mary told the children that she would come soon and take two of them to heaven, but Lucia would remain a longer time for God wished to use her to make The

Lady known and loved and to establish world devotion to her Immaculate Heart.

The fate of the children came true when Francisco died of influenza on April 4, 1918, and Jacinta died during an influenza epidemic on February 20, 1920. In about 1944, when Lucia became seriously ill, she wrote down the contents of the secret and sealed it in an envelope with instructions that it was not to be opened until 1960.

This envelope remained with the Bishop of Leira, Portugal, until 1957, when he sent it to the Vatican. It is widely supposed that Pope John XXIII opened the letter in 1960, but the contents have never been revealed.

I spent several weeks studying this most interesting and beautiful book. The many visitations are well recorded and wonderfully written along with beautiful art and colorful pictures of Mary.

On the night of August 29, 2012, I picked up the book and read the last two chapters on the visitations of Mary and was struck with awe by the information which presented in those last visitations.

In Queens, New York, from 1970, and ongoing it is reported that Mary appeared to a housewife in her home on April 7, 1970, and told Mrs. Lueken that she would appear on the grounds of a nearby church on June 18, 1970. She asked her to hold prayer vigils on that site where she also wanted a shrine dedicated to Our Lady of the Roses, Mary, Help of Mothers.

This story goes on to relate how Mrs. Lueken describes the appearances of Mary and Jesus and tells those in attendance of Mary's pronounce-ments. She told them to pray the rosary and read the Bible, but only *editions published before 1964,* to wear the brown scapula, spread the Message of Heaven and to await the return of Christ to earth, which will be soon.

Now, this got my attention! You see, I have read only one Bible since I picked it up in 1992, and read it so many times the pages came apart. That Bible is a treasure that was given to me by my dear Lillian who took care of me as a child. It has always amazed me that I never read a Bible until I was in my forties, and when I decided that I should read it, the one that I found was that grey hardcover Catholic Bible that Lilly gave me new in 1961.

My spiritual journey began and continues in this very special Bible and a used copy of it that I purchased when the original became too worn to read any longer. I am awed by the revelation that this is a Bible approved by Our Lady since it was published before 1964; and this is an extraordinary witness to its power.

Another story included towards the end of Mr. Durham's remarkable book is about a visitation of Mary to a 42 year old deaf nun in a convent in Akita, Japan in 1973. Sister Agnes was alone in a chapel looking at a 27 inch statue of Mary that had been carved by a Buddhist sculptor. On June 28, 1973, she suddenly saw light radiating from the statue and relates that "a voice of indescribable beauty struck my totally deaf ears." The voice told her that her deafness would be cured and the pain in her hand was to remind her to pray for mankind.

The sister suffered a wound in her hand and the story continues that the statue also had a cross shaped wound identical to that of Sister Agnes.

On October 13th, the voice brought her a message urging people to repent and pray the Rosary very much and their confidence in Mary will save them. It is reported on January 4, 1979, that the statue wept and continued to weep 101 times until September 15, 1981. It is also noted that samples taken of the statue's tears, blood and perspiration were tested and found to be human.

The part of this story that took my breath away was the message that was given to Sister Agnes on September 15, 1981, by her guardian angel that appeared and showed her a Bible open to God's words to the serpent in Genesis 3:15:

> *I shall put enmity between thee and the woman, and between thy seed and her seed . . .*

This is a powerful jaw-dropping, eye-popping, heart-stopping message to me! It is the very verse that set me on the path in my spiritual journey to discover that Abel was Jesus, Luluwa (twin sister of Cain) was Mary Magdalene and Eve was Mary! The poignancy of the information contained in these last two stories of Mary's visits brings such encouragement for me to continue writing and sharing my story which began in my study of the 1961 Bible and catapulted me into a new realm of information contained in lost and apocryphal books that completed the story of the first family.

I have written pages upon pages expounding the importance of the meaning of this verse. The first time I wrote about that verse is contained in my first self-published book, *A Spiritual Trilogy.* I again retell the meaning of these verses in my next book, *Trust Me, the Untold Story of Mary Magdalene.* It was from these words in Genesis that all of my theories on Jesus, Mary Magdalene and Mother Mary derive.

Now I fully realize and understand that it is time for the story of Mary to be unveiled and I know that I have been privileged and blessed by a visitation of my very own from Our Holy Mother, herself.

*Statue of Mother Mary, Infant Jesus and St.
Therese at National Shrine of St. Therese*

CHAPTER TWELVE

APOSTOLIC ANSWERS

There is yet another very important visitation of Mary to Bernadette, a young French girl who witnessed the Lady on several occasions in a cave on the banks of the Gave River near Lourdes between February and March of 1858.

This visit was especially significant in that Mary revealed to her that she was the *Immaculate Conception*.

The Church accepted and approved this visitation and the doctrine maintains that the Virgin Mary was in the first instance of her conception, preserved from all stain of original sin. The Catholic dogma also teaches that Mary ascended bodily into heaven.

Of course, the Church does not subscribe to any of my theories about the Holy Family, but they certainly acknowledge that Mary is the Immaculate Conception.

While contemplating this book about Our Lady, I prayed and called upon the Apostles to help me. After all, I thought, they above all should know the story about the Mother of Jesus since they were with her at that time.

Was I not surprised when James answered my call? My beloved Apostle James the Less is dear to my heart. I can still recall as if it were yesterday even though it was eighteen years ago the words he spoke to me. It happened one night after I had retired to my bed for the night and read the Book of James. I was so enamored by his words in the few short pages of his epistle that I closed the book and closed my eyes to think about them.

"*James your book is so wonderful that I wish you had written more,*" I said silently.

"*Sometimes less is more,*" the message was conveyed to me.

"*Of course,*" I thought, "*you are indeed James the Less to whom the Church attributes this Epistle.*"

My favorite 1961 edition of the Catholic Bible from which I always read provides an introduction to each book. In this introduction to the Catholic Epistle of St. James the Apostle there is an account as to how this book by Catholic tradition has always recognized St. James the Less as the author. It continues by describing the writer and concluding the early Fathers and councils of the Church confirm its authenticity and canonicity.

How wonderful to hear those words from the Apostle, St. James himself, telling me that sometimes *less is more*. It was a personal testament and endearment to me that he most definitely authored the book beyond any shadow of a doubt.

So to this day, among all my wonderful saints, St. James the Less holds a dear spot in my heart.

I knew before undertaking the extraordinary task of writing about the Mother of God that I would be in need of much spiritual help and guidance. That is why I called on the Apostles and I also called upon the saints, as well. This was such a daunting task, and I approached it in the same manner as I had used in finding the truth about Mary Magdalene. Just as I had prayed to Mary Magdalene for help, I first began by calling on Mother God to bring me her story and sent up petitions and prayers to the Apostles to help me since they were there during her lifetime. Surely, they would help me tell her wonderful story.

Many months have passed as I have been busy collecting information and studying about Our Lady and her many visitations recorded on the earth over centuries. She brought many messages which always showed compassion and concern for the salvation of her children.

I then went back to my old worn copy of *The Lost Books of The Bible* and *The Forgotten Books of Eden.* These books have brought me much gratification and answers to my questions that have formed while studying, reading and re-reading my favorite Bible. I recalled that these books had formed my first impression that Eve and Mary were the same person. I touched on this fact in my first writings and from there formed the undeniable conclusion that Abel returned to earth as Jesus.

In my research to discover more about the Immaculate Conception, I re-read two stories written about Mary in The Lost Books. One story is attributed to James the Less and the other is attributed to St. Matthew.

Oh, my, that makes two Apostles bringing me their stories! Thank you, and welcome Saint James and Saint Matthew.

THE GOSPEL OF THE BIRTH OF MARY

The introduction to this book explains that in primitive ages there was a Gospel extant bearing this name and attributed to St. Matthew.

The account of Mary in this book confirms Mary's message to Bernadette at Lourdes on March 25, 1858, when she told her, "I am the Immaculate Conception."

This Gospel relates that Joachim and his wife Anna lived in Nazareth and Anna was barren. They led plain and pious lives devoting their substance into three parts; to the temple, strangers and persons in poor circumstances; and the third for their own family.

They continued in this manner for about twenty years without children. They vowed that if God would favor them with a child, they would devote it to the service of the Lord.

They went every feast to the temple of the Lord, and one time the high-priest, Issachar, told Joachim that his offerings were not acceptable since God had obviously judged him unworthy to have offspring and telling him that was a curse.

Joachim was very grieved and ashamed to return home. Instead he retired to the pastures where he stayed for some time praying and fasting.

Then an angel of the Lord appeared to him to inform him that his prayers are heard and his alms ascended in the sight of God. The angel told him not to be ashamed and explained that God shuts the womb so that He may in a more wonderful manner again open it, and that which is born appear to be not the product of lust, but the gift of God.

The angel went on to describe other wondrous births to barren mothers such as Sarah, who begot Abraham a son, Isaac, in her old age; and described the barrenness of Rachel who bore Joseph, and included the mothers who bore Sampson and Samuel. The angel finished his discourse to Joachim by saying:

> *Therefore Anna your wife shall bring you a daughter, and you shall call her name Mary; she shall, according to your vow, be devoted to the Lord from her infancy, and be filled with the Holy Ghost from her mother's womb; she shall neither eat nor drink anything which is unclean, nor shall her conversation be without among the common people, but in the temple of the Lord; that so she may not fall under any slander or suspicion of what is bad.*

> *So in the process of her years, as she shall be in a miraculous manner born of one that was barren, so she shall, while yet a virgin, in a way unparalleled, bring forth the Son of*

the most High God, who shall, be called Jesus, and, according to the signification of his name, be the Saviour of all nations.

Gospel of the Birth of Mary Ch. II: 9-12

Afterwards the angel appeared to Anna saying:

Fear not, neither think that which you see is a spirit. For I am that angel who hath offered up your prayers and alms before God, and am now sent to you, that I may inform you, that a daughter will be born unto you, who shall be called Mary, and shall be blessed above all women.

She shall be, immediately upon her birth, full of the grace of the Lord, and shall continue during the three years of her weaning in her father's house, and afterwards, being devoted to the service of the Lord, shall not depart from the temple, till she arrives to years of discretion.

In a word, she shall there serve the Lord night and day in fasting and prayer, shall abstain from every unclean thing, and never know any man.

But, being an unparalleled instance without any pollution or defilement, and a virgin not knowing any man, shall bring forth a son, and a maid shall bring forth the Lord, who both by his grace and name and works shall be the Saviour of the world.

Gospel of the Birth of Mary Ch. III: 1-5

This book indeed testifies to the Immaculate Conception of Mary.

THE PROTEVANGELION

The second Lost Book that I refer to is an Historical Account of the Birth of Christ, and the Perpetual VIRGIN MARY, his Mother, by James the Lesser, cousin and brother of the Lord Jesus, Chief Apostle and first Bishop of the Christians in Jerusalem.

I marvel at the story brought by my favorite Apostle, James the Less for his story includes an account of the betrothal of Mary to Joseph and describes Joseph as an old widower with children before his marriage with the Virgin. This would, of course, account for the biblical references to Jesus having brothers and sisters. They were most certainly not children born of the Virgin Mary.

There is also the narrative about Joachim and Anna taking Mary to the temple in Jerusalem when she was three years old to fulfill their vow to dedicate her service to the Lord.

And the high-priest received her, and blessed her, and said, Mary, the Lord God hath magnified thy name to all generations, and to the very end of time by thee will the

Lord shew his redemption to the children of Israel.

And he placed her upon the third step of the altar, and the Lord gave unto her grace, and she danced with her feet, and all the house of Israel loved her."

Protevangelion, Ch. VII: 4-5

The story tells that Mary continued in the temple and received her food from the hand of an angel until she was twelve years of age. The priests wondered what to do with her lest the holy place of the Lord be defiled. So they approached Zacharias the high priest and asked him to petition the Lord on this matter. He entered into the Holy of Holies where he prayed and an angel of the Lord appeared and told him to call together all the widowers and have them bring their rods and a sign would show the husband of Mary.

The men each brought their rod to Zacharias who took them into the temple and prayed. Then when they were returned, the very last one was given to Joseph and a dove proceeded out of the rod and flew upon his head.

But Joseph refused, saying, I am an old man, and I have children, but she is young,

*and I fear lest I should appear ridiculous in
Israel.*   Protevangelion, Ch. VIII: 13

The high priest then reminded Joseph how God dealt with Dathan, Korah and Abiram when the earth opened up and swallowed them because of their contradiction.   Joseph, a God fearing man, then took Mary to his house, and departed to attend to his trade of building.

This book continues in the same vein of the scriptures and describes the angel of the Lord appearing to Mary to announce that she will conceive by the Holy Ghost and bring forth a son and name him Jesus, and he will save his people from their sins.

The remarkable part of this story is the reaction of Joseph when he returns and finds Mary six months pregnant. He is distraught that someone has committed evil in his house by seducing the Virgin.

The words of Joseph are especially poignant. In his distress over the situation, Joseph said:

*Is not the history of Adam exactly
accomplished in me?   For in the very
instant of his glory, the serpent came and
found Eve alone, and seduced her.   Just
after the same manner it has happened to
me.*"   Protevangelion Ch. X: 5

For James to relate this story delighted me since the story of the birth of Able to Eve reminds me of the very same story of the birth of Jesus to Mary and continues to confirm my belief in Eve and Mary as well as Abel and Jesus being one and the same.

Eve was pregnant when she came out of the Garden of Eden for it is written in Genesis that God spoke to her and the serpent in the garden. He said to the serpent,

"*I will place enmity between your seed and her seed.*"

God was speaking about Cain and Abel who both had been conceived in the Garden. And this conception was of a spiritual nature such as conceiving an idea. For as long as Adam and Eve were in the Garden they had spiritual natures. Thus, the seeds God refers to while speaking to Eve and the serpent is the very reference to the spiritual conception of Cain and Abel (his seed and her seed).

The difference in the conception of these sons is further demonstrated in the later conception of Seth that occurred after coming out of the Garden when Adam and Eve were changed and covered with flesh. This difference is noted in Genesis:

This is the record of the descendants of Adam. When God created man, he made him in the likeness of God. Male and female he created them, and he blessed them and called them Man when they were created. When Adam was one hundred and thirty years old, he became the father of a son in his own likeness, after his image, and he called him Seth.

Genesis 5: 1-4

The scripture describes Seth being made in Adam's likeness, not the likeness of God. Seth was born of Adam in the flesh, and not in the spiritual nature that Adam had possessed before he was put out of the Garden.

The conclusions I have drawn from my many years of study and enlightenment in regard to the story of Mary are not different from scripture, but instead are completed by the missing stories contained in the Lost Books. The salvation story does not change, it only becomes clearer.

My belief that Eve did not commit sin by eating of the forbidden fruit stems from the fact that God gave this commandment to Adam before Eve was created. This time sequence is confirmed in Genesis of the Old Testament and again in The Forgotten Books of Eden, when Adam is petitioning God, saying:

"Moreover, when Thou commandest me regarding the tree, I was neither to approach nor to eat thereof, Eve was not with me; Thou hadst not yet created her, neither hadst Thou yet taken her out of my side; nor had she yet heard this order from Thee."

First Book of Adam and Eve, Ch. XXXIV: 12-13

It goes to follow then that Eve would be the only living soul that was free from original sin and therefore, the only undefiled soul who would be worthy to return in the person of Mary, the Immaculate Conception and feminine spirit of God, who could then bring forth the Son of God by means of her own purity. Another scripture that refers to the living soul of Eve follows right after God tells Adam that the ground is cursed because of him and to dust he shall return.

This statement is set off by parentheses:

*And the man called his wife, Eve, because she was **the mother of all the living**.*

Genesis 3:20

The evidence that Eve could be the only worthy soul to mother a child of God clarifies my belief that Mary was Eve returned to earth. And this explains the spiritual and holy Immaculate Conception of Mary. Her pure soul was conceived in Anna's womb by the Holy Ghost; so Mary as Eve returned could again bring forth the true son of God, Abel, in the name of Jesus.

It also makes complete sense that Abel was the only pure child of God.   He was conceived in heaven by the Word of God to Eve when He spoke to her that He would place enmity between her seed and the serpent's seed. He attained the title of Abel the Just for his dedication to God while on the earth, and then he was murdered by his brother, Cain. Abel being a heavenly spiritual being was returned to heaven by God and the best account of this assumption is written in the Psalms.

Psalm 17 (18) is the account of a dying soul crying out to God as the breakers of death surged round about him and describes how the Lord came and drew him out of the deep waters and rescued him from the mighty enemy. It is a long Psalm that continues to tell how God rewarded him according to his justice, trained his hands for war and his arms to bend a bow of brass, subdued his enemies and stooped to make him great and head over nations.

This wonderful Psalm describes not only Jesus, but before Jesus it describes Abel the Just. This Abel the Just was the same child Mary bore and named Jesus.   The story of Eve and Abel was repeated for the salvation of mankind because God had a redemption plan from the very beginning of time. That devil that deceived Adam and Eve in the Garden was deceived in return when he put to death the Son of God. For the devil did not know there was a pure soul in the world that could not be kept in hell!

That verse in Genesis about the enmity continues in its entirety with more important information.

I will put enmity between you and the woman, between your seed and her seed;

I stopped at this semicolon, because this is the point where Abel was created by God's Word and the serpent believed God was still speaking to him. But this is not how I have read the rest of this verse. Instead of speaking to the serpent, God now directs His Word to the seed of Eve, and continues:

He shall crush your head and you shall lie in wait for his heel.

The devil hears God speak that last verse to him and believes that he, a serpent, will lie in wait for the heel of Eve's seed to crush his head.

My interpretation of this verse has been that God is now speaking to the seed that He has just planted, the seed of Abel; and God is telling Abel that he will be the one to lie in wait for the serpent's heel.

This was the amazing and outstanding hoax that did the devil in. The devil from the beginning was out to destroy the child of God for he believed that God's seed would strike him with his heel. But he heard it BACKWARDS.

If you then look at the scripture of Jesus at the Last Supper just before Judas goes out to betray him, He says:

> *But that the Scripture may be fulfilled, He who eats bread with me has lifted up his **heel against me**."*
>
> *John Ch. 13: 18-19*

So, there you find the fulfillment in the scriptures from Genesis to John. The words spoken to Abel before he was born are fulfilled in Jesus at the Last Supper before he is crucified.

Yes, it is my assumption that Abel the Just who was taken up by God likewise returned in the person of Jesus, being both Man and God; for both conceptions were spiritual in nature and both occurred to the only soul capable of conceiving spiritually, Eve created by God and returned as Mary.

Abel as Jesus also was the only living soul that was capable of this miracle since He was conceived in Eve's womb by the Word of God in heaven. And here again we find confirmation in the name of our Lord Jesus, who is described as the *Word of God*.

The old world fathers knew that Jesus would stem from the tribes of Levi and Judah and Mary's parents were of these tribes. It is written in several of the Lost Books, i.e.; the Testament of Simeon:

A priest from Levi and a King from Judah will rise.

The kingdom of heaven is like a man who sowed good seed in his field; but while men were asleep, his enemy came and sowed weeds among the wheat, and went away.

Let them both grow together until the harvest; and at harvest time I will say to the reapers, gather up the weeds first and bind them in bundles to burn; but gather the wheat into my barn.

Matthew 13: 24-30

CHAPTER THIRTEEN

BEAUTY

A theme for this book about my Mother seems to involve beauty and the appreciation of such. I was so taken by Reba's emphasis to me on how lucky I was to look so good when I was telling her I was about to become a great grandmother. She told me this two to three times while she was in the car with me. I realized that she was reminding me of her gift.

Yes, I remembered the prayers I had prayed years ago from the scriptural promises in Isaiah 61:3, that God will comfort all who mourn and give them beauty for ashes. This verse stayed with me and I believed it, of course.

One day while I was wearing a royal blue satin full-length nightgown I stopped in front of my mirror. My nightgown reminded me of the dress worn by Natalie Wood in a scene from *Gypsy*. She had just changed into that dress for her stage debut and put on white gloves that extended over her elbows. Remembering that scene and imitating her as she stood transformed from a tomboy to a beautiful woman; gazing into the full length mirror, I reached out my hand touching the glass saying, "I am a pretty girl, Mama."

These memories return as I am overwhelmed by emotion that my Mother came to remind me that she had indeed answered my prayer and to remind me that I should be appreciative of her gifts. I also know that when I reached out to the glass saying "I am a pretty girl, Mama," that it was not an idle gesture of vanity, but rather a recognition of transformation as I reached out to touch the face of God.

Believing as I do that Mary is the feminine spirit of God, it only goes to follow that she instills the beauty in all of God's creatures and creation.

I have no doubt that the lady who visited me was Mother Mary, herself. I am honored and awed by this visitation and filled with wonder for the meaning of it all. I understand and know that she has come to bring me her story. I have asked repeatedly in prayer for her to bring the story to the pages of this book, and she surely has come to do that. She has the story, and I am the fortunate scribe.

I knew Reba brought news when she asked how to get to Memorial that day on the sidewalk. I know that everything she spoke to me that day was significant and important. This book is a memorial to the grace and beauty of our heavenly Mother.

August 26, 2012

I turned on the television this morning and scrolled through the guide for something to watch and happened to see Joel Olsteen listed in the programs. I like this young handsome prosperity and positive-thinking preacher, and I was urged to see what he was talking about. I hadn't seen or heard one of his messages in a very long time, so I clicked him on.

Now, he had a message that I needed to hear about thinking large. He told how he and his wife began by getting rid of their ten inch skillet. His message was about being ready to receive the overflowing abundant gifts that God has for us by gathering lots of containers to catch the abundant blessings that had our name on it. His message also spoke about being of service to God and being obedient. I could relate to this portion of the message because every morning when I say my prayers, I do ask God to fill me and use me as I yield my vessel to Him and Her for service.

I realized that I have some work to do and I am certainly getting the messages I need to hear. I will indeed stop limiting God by limiting myself. Now, I have an outline and the work shall begin to undo my negative, limiting thoughts. After all, I have places to go, people to see and things to do. Now that is living and I plan to live large and dedicate my works to the Lord.

Two days later I had good reason to celebrate. This day I received an email from the book buyer for the Carmelite Gift Shop at the National Shrine of St. Therese. This gentleman sent the sweetest note saying he found my book, *Communion of Saints*, a *delightful read* and further saying, w*ith your strong emphasis on St. Therese of Lisieux, I think this book would be a good fit for our shop.* And he ordered copies of the book.

You can imagine my excitement! The book inspired by St. Therese, herself, was accepted at her National Shrine! I screamed and went on so that I gave myself a headache! What joy flooded my soul and heartfelt thanksgiving was extended to St. Therese and her sister Pauline, also known as Sister Agnes, for getting her book into her very own shrine; along with prayers of thanksgiving to Mother and Father God, Jesus and Mary Magdalene. This day will be a memorial day for me.

Meanwhile continuing to heed Olsteen's message to live large, I decided that my husband should take me on a trip for the Labor Day weekend. I hadn't had a vacation or trip all year and it was time for a short get away. Branson was not a long trip and we could have a dinner show and cruise on beautiful Table Rock Lake and then see Mickey Gilley's show. I got online and purchased tickets, made room reservations and the plan was all set.

It would just be a one night stay since we could drive down before the boat cruise. I recalled our last trip and thought it to be a four hour drive. Al said we should give ourselves plenty of time, but we always manage to wait until the last minute. I kept telling him it was four hours and we should leave before noon. He suggested no later than 10:00 a.m. As that morning progressed, we packed and Al told me I better print out a map to get us to the boat landing.

I mapped a route from Springfield, and then it dawned on me that it was four hours to Springfield! I had forgotten that Branson was another hour south of there. That meant we had a five hour trip ahead of us. It was 11:00 am and the boat sailed at 4 pm. Absolutely no wiggle room!

Off we went in a hurry and I kept the cruise control pegged at three miles over the speed limit. Of course, we ran into miles of road construction and Al kept telling me there was no way we would make it to the boat in time.

"Oh yes we can," I countered. "The saints are with us and we will make it! Remember how Susan and I made it back on the ship in the Mediterranean with the 80-year old priest after being lost and terribly late in Monaco?" I reminded him.

You can bet I was saying prayers to Mother Mary, Father God, Jesus, Mary Magdalene and calling on all my saints for intercession and help as I maneuvered the turnpikes toward Missouri.

We actually made the Branson exit at 3:47 pm and that number has always been special to me - so I just knew we would make it. But there were twists and turns and miles to go, we made one wrong turn, but corrected quickly as we watched the clock tick down while we headed toward the boat landing. As we approached the huge parking lot and still had to pick up our tickets at Will Call, I told Al to head for the landing while I ran ahead to get the tickets.

As I approached the dock and buildings at the landing, I heard a voice announcing, "Last Call."

I rushed toward the office and waived my paper with the reservation information his direction and hollered, "Hold the Boat!"

Then, I ran into the office and told the lady I needed my tickets quickly - and I got them. As Al approached, the young man pulled back the rope and waited for us to board the ship. When we got to our seats, the salads and drinks were waiting and the show began!

Al told me that now he believed in miracles! And since Al just turned 85 in June, and I recalled the frantic trip through Monte Carlo with the 80-year old priest, I had to wonder, *what is it about me that seems to enjoy terrorizing old men*?

EPILOGUE

MEMORIAL

At last the meaning of the message of Our Lady dawned on my conscious mind as I lay in bed in the early hours praying to her and thanking her for the many favors she has bestowed upon me. I was awake at two in the morning and my mind wandered here and there and everywhere as I recalled a multitude of random pleasant memories. One silly thought that came to mind was an afternoon as I scurried across the street downtown on my lunch hour. I was wearing the brightest yellow suit and surely surprised the black gentleman, a street person, as I abruptly crossed his path.

"Well, hello Marilyn Monroe!" he smiled at me from ear to ear.

148 Mother Who Loves You

Oh what a big happy smile I returned to him. I do love my street people and believe that saints have used this humble guise to visit us on occasion.

Then, I recalled Marilyn Monroe and her tragic death at such a young age and prayed to the Blessed Virgin Mary for her soul to be in heaven. I hoped that it was already there, but just said a few Hail Mary's for her for no particular reason. Continuing in my meandering thoughts I recalled how much my mother loved Marilyn and was so sad when she died. And my next thought about my mom was of her lying in bed praying the rosary, especially toward her last years as I helped take care of her on the weekends. I had just read earlier in my book about one of the visitations of Mary where she told someone that if a person prayed to her that person would surely be saved from the tribulation that was coming if we did not turn from our sinful ways.

It was during this train of thought that I also recalled my mother telling me, not very long before she died her special secret about the Memorare. Mom confided to me that Sister Delores when she attended St. Theresa Academy told her that this prayer was to be prayed only for very important requests of Our Lady and warned that she must not take lightly the outcome that she was seeking in this prayer. She really stressed to my mom that she must be very careful to pray for miraculous outcomes when offering this prayer to our Holy Mother, but insisted that this powerful prayer would be answered. Mom then recited it for me.

Yes, it was at this precise moment that the puzzle that had evaded me about the Lady asking for directions to Memorial exploded into my thoughts, taking me up out of the bed to write it down.

"Memorial - - - Memorare," I repeated. There is the answer to the mystery. I looked up the meaning of both words and found that *memorare* means to remember. And the definition given for *memorial* is something such as a monument or holiday, intended to celebrate or honor the memory of a person or an event.

We know the event and the person that Mary brings to memory is the terrible suffering of her Son that she witnessed in tormented sorrow as he sacrificed his life for us on the cross. Her message was contained in the name of the street for which she asked directions: Memorial.

Let us obey the requests that Our Lady has petitioned on her many visits over the centuries, and pray fervently for the salvation of all her children around the world with her extraordinary prayer as a tribute, favor and *MEMORIAL.*

MEMORARE

Remember, O most gracious Virgin Mary, that never was it known that anyone who fled to thy protection, implored thy help, or sought thine intercession was left unaided. Inspired by this confidence, I fly unto thee, O Virgin of virgins, my mother; to thee do I come, before thee I stand, sinful and sorrowful. O Mother of the Word Incarnate, despise not my petitions, but in thy mercy hear and answer me. Amen.

To this day I can recite every prayer I learned growing up in the Catholic Church, but the Memorare always evades me. I sometimes think it is because it is not to be recited mindlessly, but prayed very seriously. After all, I am reminded of my own mother's warning not to use this prayer except in very special circumstances and for very important requests. My mother was very serious, for I was almost sixty years old before she confided in me the importance of this very special prayer.

My mother brings to mind such strong emotions of love and these memories combine with the very voice of God, when I heard Her speak to me in my own mother's voice, saying:

Anne, I have always been there for you.

Yes, Mother God spoke to me those words immediately after I heard God Father's voice speak to me the words of this book:

I am the Father who created you and
THE MOTHER WHO LOVES YOU.

Your throne, O God, stands forever and ever; a tempered rod is your royal scepter. You love justice and hate wickedness; therefore God, your God has anointed you with the oil of gladness above your fellow kings. With myrrh and aloes and cassia your robes are fragrant; from ivory palaces string music brings you joy. The daughters of kings come to meet you; the queen takes her place at your right hand in gold of Ophir.

Psalm 44:7

WORDS FROM THE AUTHOR

THE OCTOBER SURPRISE

Synchronicities are amazing events that jump up and shout "Here I Am!" They are earth shaking, undeniable coincidences that come together to create change. I am in the midst of a current series of these synchronicities and the excitement of actually recognizing that the Universe does come together to promote my heart's desires is astonishing. Bur, actually, it isn't odd at all.

We want to believe that God loves us and desires to shower us with blessings, but they so easily escape us because we continue to control our destiny out of fear.

Trust is a confidence that is not easy to extend. Fear, on the other hand, is a lack of confidence that keeps us bound to worldly realities as we understand them.

We believe in God but we fail to understand just how much God loves us. It is our own judgment of unworthiness that becomes a physical blockage to the abundant blessings of God. *Let go and let God* sounds so easy, yet with great difficulty do we practice it.

Rather than try to explain the intangible aspects of trust, I will instead share some of the events that brought me to the undeniable recognition that things were happening outside my control and in line with my desires.

I am a creature of change and also a creature of habit which brings much conflict. I'm sure I am not alone in these conflicting feelings. As a creature of change, I enjoy moving around, meeting new people, and starting off on new adventures. As a creature of habit, I find myself burrowing into a rut of repetitiveness that becomes boring, but safe.

Oh, how I envy the entrepreneurs, those brave souls who strive to do the work that satisfies the soul. That is not the safe route, for sure, but it is truly the happy road to success. The rest of us find our security in a job where we can count on a regular paycheck to get us through life. This is the safe road to boredom, for sure.

Not all of us are daredevils and some are quite content, but I am not that person. I can stay in a secure place for a few years, usually three, and then I know it is time for me to make a change. I'm not very brave though, because I only move to a new and similar position, but it affords another temporary change and adventure as I meet new people and conquer new challenges.

That is where I am today, five years at the same job and though I like the work and the people I work with, my soul is restless for a change of scenery and activity.

My latest and very exciting synchronicity came recently when in prayer I asked God to surprise me. I always pray every morning, sometimes to offer thanks and sometimes to hold up special prayer requests. I don't believe I ever asked God to just surprise me with blessings. Well, Surprise! It is just days before our next presidential election and the news is full of the possibility of an *October surprise* event that might swing the votes to one of the candidates.

God answered my prayer with my own October surprise.

I recently had thoughts about a dear friend and attorney that I used to work for. She is my daughter's age and a beautiful girl. For some reason I had been thinking of her over this weekend and to my surprise she sent me an email saying the same thing. She had been thinking about me at the same time. Coincidence?

In response I casually asked if she knew anyone that might be looking for a person with my skill as I felt it was time for me to make a change.

"How about office manager at my firm?" came the totally unexpected answer!

Wow - this was a lot to consider. This was both a change in my position and location. I was in a downtown law firm; and her firm was in Bricktown a half mile east. Was I really ready for a change? Could I deny the synchronicity going on here? Even my friend who made the offer was surprised when I agreed to take the job. But, then again she reads my books and she has her own awareness going on. Enlightened persons get results!

This was indeed an October surprise that I am sure is going to effect a big change in my circumstances. I am so excited because this is a real answer to prayer that came when I wasn't looking for it, and because I wasn't looking - - it came through!

A confirmation of my decision to make a change dawned on me when I realized the date that I accepted the new position was the same day my finger injury began on October 25th, one year ago to the day. Even more incredible, my unexpected start date landed on November 8, 2012; the first anniversary of the day that I reported my finger injury on November 8, 2011.

I had an even better October surprise on October 1, 2012. My great-grandson was born and he came on the Feast Day of my beautiful patron saint, Therese of Lisieux.

Welcome, Malakai!

It is so interesting to re-read the pages of this book and discover the meaningful events and synchronicities that occurred this past year. It happens over and over when I write, but I am always taken by surprise and delighted each time my book comes to life and takes me on another wondrous journey. My saints are always close and I still believe St. Therese guides my pen (or keyboard) when I write. I just need to hold on and pay attention. The timing is always so perfect.

These very significant events occurred while this book was in progress in 2012; and they relate to the very heavenly ladies that were featured in my last three books:

July 22 - Feast Day of Mary Magdalene:
Mother Mary, Our Lady, visited me.

October 1 - Feast Day of St. Therese of Lisieux:
My great-grandson was born.

January 1 - Feast Day of Mother Mary:
This book was completed.

I am still looking for that shower of blessings that I described at the beginning of my book when I compared my troubles to Job. Well, it is with great confidence that I believe the first drops of that shower have begun to fall.

ABOUT THE AUTHOR

Anne Urne on transatlantic crossing from the French Riviera where she visited the grotto of Mary Magdalene in Provence. It was at the grotto entrance high atop the mountain that she found the beautiful statue that graces the cover of this book. While looking through cruise photos for a cover picture, Anne knew immediately this one had been waiting for her. This Pieta is different than most because Mary Magdalene is weeping at the feet of Mary holding Jesus and it makes the perfect cover for the story of Mary and her children.

Ms. Urne lives in Oklahoma with her husband and continues to write. She is a member of the NFPW, National Federation of Press Women, and the IWPA, Illinois Women's Press Association. She loves traveling to literary festivals. Her favorite venue is the Chicago Tribune's Printers Row Literary Festival which she attends each June signing her books. She also enjoys spiritual adventures with her cousin, Susan, as they travel around the world.

It is no surprise to Anne that her books lean toward the importance of the feminine role in religious and spiritual history since she came of age during the movement that ushered in the Equal Rights Amendment.

Anne Urne with her younger sister was raised by her widowed mother in a middle-class Irish, Catholic household in Illinois. She has been a medical and legal secretary, paralegal, civilian safety officer for the Air Force, a campaign scheduler for Democratic campaigns for Lt. Governor, Governor, U.S. Congressional and Senate candidates, worked for two Speakers of the Oklahoma House of Representatives and the first woman Chief Justice of the Oklahoma Supreme Court. Her career also included extensive travel across the country for over a decade assisting her catastrophe adjuster husband with property damage inspections from the Northridge Earthquake to Katrina. Anne is longtime student of Scripture, Apocrypha, various religious traditions, mysticism and spirituality, an author and a publisher.

Anne Urne began her spiritual quest in 1992 when she picked up the Bible given to her as a child by her devoted babysitter, Lillian. It was at her house in Illinois that Anne always admired the picture of St. Therese, the Little Flower, and a few years later chose St. Therese as her patron saint for her Confirmation. Anne credits St. Therese of Lisieux for her remarkable spiritual journey.

In 2000 she began recording wonderful insights that came to her from years of study and these evolved into her books. She completed each small book at Christmas. She later published some of these in *A Spiritual Trilogy.*

In 2004 she completed the fourth book of her journey entitled: Trust Me, The Untold Story of Mary Magdalene, in which she solved the mystery stirred up by Dan Brown's famous Da Vinci Code with her amazing story that sheds a whole new light on the meaning of the relationship between Mary Magdalene and Jesus.

Anne's next book, *Communion of Saints Inspired by St. Therese,* brings a new dynamic to Anne's books. This is a mystical achievement as St. Therese brings her continuing story of a soul's journey into this extraordinary adventure. Anne Urne with her cousin, Susan, travel the world and Anne describes the wondrous presence and help of the saints who come to her aid. You will marvel at the spiritual messages conveyed to her as she communes with the saints and learns that just as St. Therese always believed, heaven can be found on earth and there can be communion with the saints. A truly inspiring message that only the saints could bring and a tribute to the devotion and hard work of dedicated nuns who are responsible for bringing us some of the greatest spiritual classics.

Anne's latest book, *The Mother Who Loves You,* is her third book and the crown jewel in her books about holy women. Anne had been suffering some physical maladies in 2012, and the book seemed to be languishing; UNTIL by a stroke of magic it came to life toward the end of December and surprised her by finishing on the very Feast Day of Mother Mary - New Year's Day 2013. *Happy New Year, Mother! This is your story and it is beautiful!*

Anne says that her books always seem to take on a life of their own and she is both surprised and amazed at the stories that pour forth onto the pages of her books. She is very grateful for her spiritual mentor and guide, St. Therese of Lisieux.

The Catholic Church ascribes certain mysteries to be meditated upon while praying the Rosary. They are the Joyful, Luminous, Sorrowful and Glorious Mysteries.

In the course of her spiritual journey Anne was shown the importance of the feminine role in the story of creation and salvation. It took two entities, male and female, to form the perfect union that would restore the original creation to the image of God, male and female.

In that vein, Anne shares her own personal mysteries from the Bible which she uses to pray the Rosary to demonstrate the importance of both male and female as described in the relationship between Mary Magdalene and Jesus.

THE MARY MAGDALENE MYSTERIES

1. The Wedding at Cana;
2. Bathing the feet of Jesus with her tears and wiping them with her beautiful hair;
3. Anointing Jesus with fragrant expensive nard from *an urn;*
4. Witnessing the Crucifixion of Jesus; and
5. Being the first to witness His Resurrection.

Mother Mary was present for most of these events.

Special thanks to FULL CIRCLE BOOKSTORE at 50 Penn Place in Oklahoma City who host all of the first book signings for Anne Urne. It is a great place to find a copy of Anne's books nestled among more than 60,000 new titles in the largest independent, locally owned, general interest bookstore in Oklahoma.

BIBLIOGRAPHY

New American Catholic Edition THE HOLY BIBLE
Douay version and Confraternity of Christian Doctrine.
Imprimatur: Francis Cardinal Spellman, Archbishop of
New York, NY, June 8, 1961
His Holiness Pope Pius XII - Urges the Study of
the Sacred Scriptures
Holy Father Pope Leo XIII - Encyclical Letter

© 1950, 1958, 1961, by Benziger Brothers

1961 Author given this book by Lillian James in
Decatur, IL
1993 Author first read entire book on 2/24/93 in
Walters, OK and continued reading from cover to
cover 19 more times through 5/10/96 while
traveling around the country

A SPIRITUAL TRILOGY
©2003 by Anne Urne, BOIS Publications
2011 2nd Printing

2003 First published book by, Anne Urne; included
were her first 3 books written and completed in:
2000 Way Beyond the River
2001 The Walls Came Tumbling Down
2002 It Came to Pass

TRUST ME
The Untold Story of Mary Magdalene
© 2004 by Anne Urne and Published by BOIS
Publications
2011 2nd Printing

www.ingramcontent.com/pod-product-compliance
Lightning Source LLC
Chambersburg PA
CBHW060857280326
41934CB00007B/1087